Strategic Defense Initiative

About the Book and Editors

Intended for use as a text in courses on national security, arms control, and peace studies, this collection of statements by world leaders and eminent scholars offers an accurate and comprehensive guide through the maze of claims and criticisms about "Star Wars," the sensationally controversial effort of the Reagan administration to reorient U.S. nuclear strategy to strategic defense.

The contents include a thorough introduction by the editors and individual chapters outlining the strategic defense initiative as originally conceived and subsequently modified by the Reagan administration; the arguments for and against the plan's strategic and technical feasibility; and assessments of the harmful and constructive effects of strategic defense on U.S.-Soviet and U.S.-allied relations.

P. Edward Haley is director of the Keck Center for International Strategic Studies and chairman of the International Relations Committee, Claremont McKenna College. He has worked on the staffs of members of the U.S. Senate and House of Representatives and was an international affairs Fellow of the Council on Foreign Relations. **Jack Merritt** is professor emeritus of physics, Claremont McKenna College. Prior to coming to Claremont, he served as an administrative officer at the U.S. Atomic Energy Commission and the National Science Policy Organization of the Bureau of Budget.

Strategic Defense Initiative
Folly or Future?

edited by P. Edward Haley
and Jack Merritt

Westview Press / **Boulder and London**

358.1754
S898

Copyright © 1986 by Westview Press, Inc.

Published in 1986 in the United States of America by Westview Press, Inc.; Frederick A. Praeger, Publisher; 5500 Central Avenue, Boulder, Colorado 80301

Library of Congress Cataloging-in-Publication Data
Strategic defense initiative.
  Bibliography: p.
  Includes index.
  1. Strategic Defense Initiative. I. Haley, P. Edward.
II. Merritt, Jack.
UG743.S776   1986   358'.1754   86-7810
ISBN 0-8133-0414-8
ISBN 0-8133-0415-6 (pbk.)

Printed and bound in the United States of America

The paper used in this publication meets the requirements of the American National Standard for Permanence of Paper for Printed Library Materials Z39.48-1984.

10   9   8   7   6   5   4   3   2   1

Contents

Preface.. ix

Introduction: Strategic Defense, Nuclear Deterrence, and Arms
    Control, *P. Edward Haley and Jack Merritt* 1
Bibliography: Introduction 19

PART ONE
THE REAGAN STRATEGIC
DEFENSE INITIATIVE

1. Address to the Nation on the Strategic Defense Initiative,
    Ronald Reagan 23

2. Ballistic Missile Defenses and U.S. National Security,
    Fred S. Hoffman...27

3. On the Road to a More Stable Peace, *Paul H. Nitze*...........37

4. Statement to Congress, *Lt. General James A. Abrahamson*......43

Bibliography: Part One...51

PART TWO
STRATEGIC FEASIBILITY

5. BMD and Strategic Instability, *George Rathjens*
    and Jack Ruina 55

6. The President's Choice: Star Wars or Arms Control,
    McGeorge Bundy, George F. Kennan,
    Robert S. McNamara, and Gerard Smith 65

7. The Case for Strategic Defense: An Option for a World
    Disarmed, *George A. Keyworth II*.............................73

8. A Case for Strategic Defense, *Colin S. Gray* 81

Bibliography: Part Two 89

PART THREE
TECHNICAL FEASIBILITY

9. The SDI: A Technical Appraisal, *Sidney D. Drell, Philip J. Farley, and David Holloway* 93

10. Is SDI Technically Feasible? *Harold Brown* 109

11. The Strategic Defense Initiative: Defensive Technologies Study, *James C. Fletcher* 119

12. SDI: The Last, Best Hope, *Edward Teller* 127

Bibliography: Part Three 131

PART FOUR
SDI AND U.S.-SOVIET RELATIONS

13. Nuclear Disarmament by the Year 2000, *Mikhail S. Gorbachev* 135

14. The Strategic Defense Initiative and the Soviet Union, *David Holloway* 139

15. Report to Congress After Geneva Summit, *Ronald Reagan* 151

16. The Nuclear and Space Arms Talks: Where We Are After the Summit, *Paul H. Nitze* 155

Bibliography: Part Four................................161

PART FIVE
SDI AND U.S.-ALLIED RELATIONS

17. Strategic Defense and the Western Alliance, *Christoph Bertram* 165

18. Defence and Security in the Nuclear Age, *Sir Geoffrey Howe*....173

19. Statement to the Bundestag, *Helmut Kohl* 179

20. Press Conference, *Margaret Thatcher* 183

Bibliography: Part Five 187

Glossary..189
About the Contributors 191

Preface

The purpose of this collection of articles is to make available to students, scholars, analysts, military leaders, and policymakers in this country and abroad the information they require in order to understand and develop their own views of the Reagan administration's Strategic Defense Initiative (SDI). The selections included in the text have been chosen to present the best argued and most representative opinions for and against SDI.

As with our earlier *Nuclear Strategy, Arms Control, and the Future,* which has happily been well received and widely adopted, we have acted in part to meet the needs of our students to have readily available a set of authoritative readings on major nuclear issues.

The development and publication of this book also reflect the continuing concern of the Keck Center for International Strategic Studies to contribute to the debate on questions concerning the central balance between the Soviet Union and the United States and the future of nuclear arms control.

We recognize that our readers may have found articles that they regard as more helpful in understanding one or another of the issues pertaining to SDI, and we welcome their suggestions.

The collaboration of Haley and Merritt continues to be a fruitful and pleasant one in class and in research and preparation of these and related studies.

We thank Miriam Gilbert, director of the College Division of Westview Press, for her continued support and interest in our work, and Jackie Melvin of the Keck Center for her assistance with the editorial tasks involved in completing the manuscript.

P. Edward Haley
Jack Merritt

Introduction: Strategic Defense, Nuclear Deterrence, and Arms Control

When he announced the Strategic Defense Initiative (SDI) on March 23, 1983, President Ronald Reagan held out the prospect of the abolition of nuclear weapons. "Isn't it worth every investment necessary," he asked, "to free the world from the threat of nuclear war?"

It would not be a simple matter to abolish the balance of terror. The president challenged U.S. scientists to lead the way: "I call upon the scientific community in our country, those who gave us nuclear weapons, to turn their great talents now to the cause of mankind and world peace, to give us the means of rendering these nuclear weapons impotent and obsolete." In the meantime, the United States would maintain offensive nuclear deterrence and seek negotiated arms reductions with the Soviet Union.

AMBIGUITIES OF THE SDI STRATEGY

The proposal, popularly known as Star Wars, instantly provoked a controversy not only in the United States but among allied governments and peoples and in the Soviet Union. The intensity of the reaction resulted from the strategic implications of the president's plan and from the daunting complexity of an undertaking to erect a missile-proof shield over the United States and its allies.

Critics and supporters of SDI alike were troubled by the administration's apparent turn away from the strategy of offensive nuclear deterrence. Deterrence is an attempt to prevent aggression by threatening to use nuclear weapons against an aggressor. The threat carries a warning that the losses inflicted will outweigh any benefits that might be won. The concept of deterrence, and the weapons and doctrine elaborated from it, has dominated nuclear strategy since 1945. Although the strategy of offensive nuclear deterrence is full of ambiguity and risk, its longevity lends a kind of familiarity and seeming predictability to the conflict between the Soviet Union and the United States. The possibility of upsetting the reign of offensive deterrence was bound to stir dissent and concern.

On the technical side, no one knew in 1983 whether the president's SDI could be built and no one knows today. The exotic technologies involved, such as high-power lasers, giant mirrors in space, electromagnetically accelerated projectiles, and extraordinarily complex computer programs, are either in their infancy or have yet to be developed. However, the astounding scope and pace of scientific and technological breakthroughs in the past century have made scientists and engineers understandably wary of predicting the impossibility of inventing anything. Even so, many scientists doubt that the weapons required for SDI can be made to work. Others doubt that it will be possible to create and make reliable the fantastically complex computer programs needed to detect thousands of incoming warheads from decoys and to aim and fire the weapons. With his address and his subsequent multi-billion-dollar funding requests and organized research and development program, the president appeared to take a step into the unknown on a subject of enormous human and political significance.

The Strategic Defense Initiative calls for the use of new technologies to destroy attacking missiles and warheads before they reach their targets. Sensors in space would track enemy missiles from the instant they were launched. The most advanced computers and software programs would aim and guide a sophisticated combination of defenses—possibly including such weapons as chemical and X-ray lasers (driven by nuclear explosions), electromagnetic guns, and particle beams—against an enemy's attack during four general stages or layers:

- *Boost Intercept.* The first three to five minutes of flight, while the rocket engines are firing, before the bus carrying the reentry vehicles separates from its missile booster and before the missile reaches 200 to 300 kilometers in altitude. (A bus is a vehicle with its own thrusters that maneuvers and drops each warhead into its assigned trajectory; a reentry vehicle is a device to carry warheads, the explosive part of a missile.)
- *Post-Boost Intercept.* The next five to 10 minutes of flight, from approximately 200 to 1,000 kilometers in altitude, during the time that the reentry vehicles separate from the bus carrying them.
- *Midcourse Intercept.* Fifteen to 20 minutes in flight, after the reentry vehicles have separated from the bus.
- *Terminal Intercept.* The last minute or so of flight, as the reentry vehicles reenter the atmosphere.

Through this defense in depth the president seeks to eliminate the threat of massive strategic nuclear attack against civilians. There can be no other meaning to his rhetorical question: "What if free people could live secure in the knowledge that their security did not rest upon the threat of instant U.S. retaliation to deter a Soviet attack, that we could intercept and destroy strategic ballistic missiles before they reached our own soil or that of our allies?"

The president scrupulously warned that such a goal could not be achieved quickly or easily: "I know this is a formidable, technical task. . . . It will take years, probably decades of efforts on many fronts." He also repeatedly emphasized that he was launching a novel program of research: "I am directing a comprehensive and intensive effort to define a long-term research and development program to begin to achieve our ultimate goal of eliminating the threat posed by strategic nuclear missiles."

OPPOSITION TO AND DEFENSE OF SDI

Reagan's warnings that SDI would take time and involve a revolutionary approach did not diminish the opposition. The core of the president's plan—a space-based shield against nuclear attack—aroused anger, disbelief, and fervent opposition. Allied governments in Western Europe were openly skeptical. The Soviet government and many Western proponents of arms control rushed to challenge the plan. On the technical side, the defense initiative will not work, they said; SDI cannot be made leakproof. Because of the destructiveness of nuclear weapons, if even a few warheads hit cities, the results would be catastrophic. An attacker can easily fool and overwhelm the defenses by adding warheads and decoys to its nuclear offense. The proposed defensive systems themselves would be delicate, fragile, and vulnerable to attack in space, and perhaps not even technically feasible. They would be enormously costly, and their pursuit would waste resources that could be better spent in other areas of defense, such as conventional readiness and force improvements.

Politically, SDI will poison U.S.-Soviet relations, critics say, and increase the risk of nuclear war. The present condition of mutual, stable deterrence will be undermined and replaced with uncertainty and ambiguity. Because implementing SDI will violate the Anti-Ballistic Missile (ABM) Treaty, the United States will trigger a massive offensive nuclear arms race, as each superpower rushes to counter the other's possible successes at defense. SDI will destroy the North Atlantic alliance (NATO), an essential part of U.S. security, because the Europeans will fear a dilution of the U.S. commitment to defend them once the United States is safe behind its defensive shield.

The administration and the supporters of SDI have replied that the critics are overly pessimistic. Great progress has been made in recent years in developing the necessary exotic technologies. For example, under test conditions a defensive missile has intercepted the warhead of an intercontinental ballistic missile in flight. Research in lasers is moving much more rapidly than expected. SDI's concept of layered defense goes far to solve the problem of "leakage"—missiles penetrating the shield. No single layer of the defense needs to be perfect. If each of four independent layers of defense is 90 percent effective, all but 1 of 10,000 attacking warheads will be destroyed. Most important, supporters insist that without SDI the United

States can give no answer to the threat to its land-based missiles posed by improvements in the accuracy and destructiveness of Soviet nuclear forces since the early 1970s. As for the vulnerability and cost of the defensive systems, the administration has argued that it will not deploy a system that is not cost-effective at the margin—that costs less to build than to counter—and is relatively invulnerable against attack.

In the five parts of this book we have presented the most important arguments to date for and against SDI. The parts cover the Reagan administration's original proposal, together with the modifications accepted since March 1983; the main disagreements about strategic and technical feasibility; the effects of SDI on relations between the United States and the Soviet Union; and the effects of SDI on relations between the United States and its allies.

Two issues touched upon in this book—the effects of SDI on nuclear strategy and on U.S.-Soviet relations—are so important that we will devote special attention to them in this introduction. Specifically, what effects will SDI have on the maintenance of offensive nuclear deterrence by the Western democracies? And what effects will SDI have on the prospects for further progress on nuclear arms control between the Soviet Union and the United States?

SDI AND OFFENSIVE NUCLEAR DETERRENCE

Throughout history there has been an oscillation between offensive and defensive dominance in strategy and warfare. In World War I, for example, barbed wire, machine guns, and heavy artillery gave the defense the upper hand. During World War II the mobility and shock effects of massed tank attacks restored the edge to the offense. The development of nuclear bombs and intercontinental missiles prolonged the dominance of the offense. The Reagan administration's SDI challenges this pattern. Is defense making a comeback? The proponents of SDI say "Yes!" Its critics disagree. Part of the bitterness in the SDI debate stems precisely from disagreements about whether in our nuclear age, characterized by policies of offensive deterrence and the threat of mutual destruction, it is logical and safe to try to defend people against nuclear attack and risk upsetting the balance of terror. At issue is the essence of offensive nuclear deterrence as it has been understood and practiced in the United States for thirty years.

Strategic Defense and Assured Destruction

During the Eisenhower (1953–1961), Kennedy (1961–1963), and Johnson administrations (1963–1969), strategic defense was taken seriously in Congress, the White House, and the Pentagon. The deployment of defenses against bombers and missiles was politically popular. The American people thought and still think that it is natural for the government to try to protect them against nuclear attack. Moreover, the large defense contractors who would benefit from the research and construction contracts heartily supported the idea for scientific as well as business reasons. Research funds were regularly provided, and limited deployments of antiaircraft missiles were made.

Some members of the executive branch had serious reservations about strategic defense. Eisenhower worried most about the cost. However, the Congress was willing to pay, and cost was not the decisive reason for hesitation about defenses. Robert McNamara, who served as secretary of defense for both President John Kennedy and President Lyndon Johnson, and his advisers worried most about the strategic disadvantages of defense against nuclear attack. McNamara's argument was simple: Cities cannot be protected against nuclear attack because if just one nuclear bomb penetrates the defensive shield there will still be a catastrophe. Worse, if one side begins to deploy defenses on a large scale, the other side will greatly increase its offensive missiles and simply overwhelm the defense. That was the U.S. counterapproach when it became concerned about the antimissile defenses constructed by the Soviet Union around Moscow. McNamara believed that if one or both superpowers attempted to create defenses against nuclear attack, the net result would be vast increases in expenditures on both offensive and defensive weaponry without any appreciable gain in security.

McNamara's opposition to strategic defense was consistent with his preferred offensive nuclear strategy of assured destruction. According to McNamara, the United States could deter an attack on itself and its allies by maintaining the ability to inflict "unacceptable damage" on any attacker— specifically the Soviet Union—even after having suffered the worst possible first strike. U.S. cities would be left undefended as proof that the United States planned no aggressive attacks against the Soviet Union. McNamara hoped that the achievement of parity by the Soviet Union would lead to its recognition and acceptance of assured destruction. Then the two governments could agree to significantly reduce their offensive nuclear forces.

McNamara lost the first battles about strategic defense. Late in the Johnson administration the Congress voted and the president agreed to deploy a "thin" defense that would have partially protected U.S. intercontinental ballistic missile (ICBM) silos and some major cities. Construction began on a system of missile defense based on the long-range, high-altitude nuclear-tipped Spartan missile and the shorter range, high-speed Sprint missile. Since leaving office McNamara has made clear that the administration decided to deploy an ABM system in response to political demands from the Congress that President Johnson felt obliged to accommodate. McNamara believed then and continues to believe that on strategic and logical grounds the United States must not defend itself against nuclear attack.

ABM Treaty

Although McNamara lost the battle about antiballistic missile defense (ABM) (as strategic defense was then known), his position was adopted by the administrations of Richard Nixon (1969–1974), Gerald Ford (1974–1977), and Jimmy Carter (1977–1981). Richard Nixon and Leonid Brezhnev signed a treaty on the limitation of antiballistic missile systems (ABM Treaty) on

May 26, 1972, in Moscow. After receiving the consent of the Senate, President Nixon ratified the treaty, and it entered into force on October 3, 1972.

The ABM Treaty severely curtailed the deployment of missile defenses by the Soviet Union and the United States. Both sides were allowed to build ABM systems in two areas, with an operating radius of 150 kilometers around one intercontinental ballistic missile (ICBM) field and around the national capital. No more than 100 ABM launchers and 100 interceptor missiles and no more than two large phased-array radars and 18 ABM radars could be built at each site. In 1974 the two governments reduced the allowable ABM systems to one for each side. According to the ABM Treaty the missiles and radars could not be used to provide nationwide defense.

In keeping with its strategy of assured destruction, the United States chose to defend an ICBM missile field at Grand Forks Air Force Base in North Dakota. Subsequently, the United States decided not to build even this limited defense. Consistent with its war-winning strategy, the Soviet Union chose to defend Moscow, its national command center. Because both sides had declined to try to defend all their cities, many observers in the West saw their mutual vulnerability to nuclear attack as a cornerstone of the strategic relationship between the Soviet Union and the United States. To its many supporters, the ABM Treaty came to symbolize the possibility that despite their differences the two adversaries could agree on matters of fundamental importance. Large amounts of money were saved on both sides because both were able to skip a nationwide deployment of defensive systems that would not have worked and were already being overtaken by technological change. The strategic relationship gained an element of predictability and continuity, even as it was being convulsed by dramatic improvements in the accuracy of multiple independently targeted reentry vehicles (MIRVs).

SDI: Strategic Revolution

As these developments make clear, President Reagan's SDI proposal touched issues of fundamental importance. He did not suggest a change in emphasis or weaponry but a strategic revolution. His proposal denied the primacy of offensive nuclear deterrence. This approach was troubling because no one had worked through the logic of strategic defense. The administration spoke confidently of "deterrence by denial" of victory. But would an enemy be deterred from launching a nuclear attack by the apparent effectiveness of an opponent's antimissile defenses? Would not the threat of offensive nuclear reprisal also be required to make deterrence work? Moreover, what if the Soviet Union chose to increase its offensive nuclear arsenal and began a determined effort to produce and deploy its own strategic defense systems? Presumably, the United States would also have to respond with a matching offensive build-up. How would SDI affect deterrence in circumstances in which both sides had greatly expanded their offensive arsenals and had major defensive systems in place?

In response to these doubts, the administration and the supporters of SDI, such as the lobby group High Frontier, pointed to four factors that have worked to reawaken the U.S. government's interest in strategic defense: (1) perceived changes in the military balance that developed in the 1970s in favor of the Soviet Union over the United States, particularly Soviet deployment of thousands of large, extremely accurate warheads on its ICBMs; the U.S. delay, following its assured-destruction approach, of a response in kind for a decade; (2) the severe decline in popular support in the Western democracies for the maintenance of offensive nuclear deterrence and the modernization of the weapons on which it depends; (3) a technological advantage in favor of the United States over the Soviet Union in the development of the esoteric technologies on which SDI must rely; and (4) a growing disenchantment within the executive branch and among an influential group of defense intellectuals with the established view of nuclear strategy, arms control, and Soviet-U.S. relations.

Of these, only the third—a presumed U.S. technological advantage— can be easily rebutted. The belief that the United States can outperform the Soviet Union in the esoteric technologies of SDI is widespread in the United States and abroad. In the short term it is probably true, and its greatest importance may be in the area of computerized information processing necessary to acquire targets, discriminate real from decoy warheads, and aim and coordinate defensive fire. In the longer term, the advantage is much less impressive. Since 1945 the Soviet Union has repeatedly shown that it can match and sometimes surpass the United States in the development of nuclear offensive and defensive capabilities. That the United States systems are more compact or sophisticated has only a limited value; no rewards are given for elegance in this contest, only for competence.

Soviet War-Winning Strategy

Although Robert McNamara's position on ABM and assured destruction became strategic gospel in the United States, his views on nuclear strategy and the strategic relationship were not adopted by the Soviet government. One must be careful in describing the differences between the Soviet and U.S. approaches; it is easy to be misled by the partisans of the different interpretations. The Soviet government has adopted a war-winning nuclear strategy. This does not mean that the Soviet leaders wish to wage a nuclear war. They wish to achieve their objectives without such a war. However, in the event of war Soviet military doctrine envisions the widescale and early use of nuclear weapons. The Soviet government has organized its forces and tried to protect its leadership, people, and industry with victory in mind to a much greater degree than has the United States.

The Soviet government has agreed to leave its cities vulnerable to U.S. missiles and has in most ways abided by the ABM treaty. The location and purpose of a radar complex near Krasnoyarsk in central Russia, which has been photographed by U.S. spy satellites are widely considered to be in violation of the ABM Treaty. According to the treaty large radar complexes of this kind are supposed to be installed near the frontiers and directed outward instead of located in the center of the country where they can be integrated into a nationwide strategic defense system. Some U.S. analysts also question whether the newer antiaircraft defenses deployed by the Soviet Union do not also have a capability against intercontinental and tactical ballistic missiles. In its report, *Soviet Military Power 1985*, the U.S. Defense Department identified the Soviet surface-to-air missiles SA-10 and SA-X-12 (now being flight tested) as possibly capable of intercepting U.S. strategic missiles and the SA-X-12 as a weapon that may be able to engage the U.S. tactical missiles stationed in Europe, which include the Lance, Pershing I, and Pershing II.

But these are not the main issues; the decisive issue is the Soviet calculation that as its strategic offensive forces have grown, the United States has become less and less inclined to resort to its assured-destruction capability. In particular, the United States can no longer assume that extended deterrence—the protection of allies against attack by the threat of nuclear reprisal—would prevent aggression.

If at this point the Soviet Union had adopted McNamara's standard of assured destruction and had built a large number of relatively inaccurate weapons, useful only in threatening to attack cities and industrial concentrations, the United States might have avoided some of the problems of deterrence and extended deterrence. Instead the Soviet government replaced the missiles with which they had overtaken the United States with new ICBMs that carry MIRVs capable of destroying the land-based missiles of the United States.

The Soviets forced a strategic dilemma on the United States: In a crisis the United States could not risk attacking Soviet cities because that would bring a Soviet response against U.S. cities. But U.S. land- and sea-based missiles were not sufficiently accurate to avoid causing great loss of life among civilians and destruction of industry and natural resources in the Soviet Union (collateral damage), even if U.S. nuclear weapons were used against military targets. By this logic, if the Soviet Union used its highly accurate MIRVs to strike at U.S. ICBMs and avoided cities, the United States would be powerless to respond for fear of bringing about attacks on its cities.

Faced with this dilemma, the United States decided to copy the Soviet approach and deploy large numbers of highly accurate weapons—the MX and Trident D-5 missiles, air-, ground-, and sea-launched cruise missiles— that could destroy missiles in hardened silos and would cause relatively less collateral damage. SDI was born in part as another response to the loophole that Soviet leaders believed they had found in U.S. strategy because it promised to block the Soviet capability to destroy U.S. ICBMs.

Decline of Public Support for Deterrence

The decline in popular support for offensive nuclear deterrence in the Western democracies and in particular for the replacement of existing weapons with more modern ones also contributed to the Reagan administration's decision to initiate SDI. Although the passionate outburst of antinuclear sentiment in the Western democracies in the early 1980s has died down, it is important to recall the miles-long human chains of protesters in Europe and the rash of New England town meetings declaring their cities to be nuclear-free zones. In many ways, the Reagan administration's provocative rhetoric on arms control and U.S.-Soviet relations swelled the ranks and intensity of the opposition. Facing strong and growing protests, particularly in West Germany and Great Britain but not negligible in the United States, the administration changed course and began to speak and act as if arms control held an important place on its agenda. The Reagan administration obviously concluded that it would be easier to convince its own citizens and the world at large of its peaceful intentions if it changed its approach to arms control and put forward SDI.

In regard to arms control the administration realized that it must try to split the antinuclear activists from the "ordinary citizens" (those with moderate opinions) whose attraction to the protests had given them the mass needed to upset public opinion within NATO. Antinuclear activists demand that the leaders of the Western democracies must achieve immediate and massive reductions in nuclear weapons. A few even seek total nuclear disarmament. The ordinary citizens of NATO countries, who had begun to join the protests by the thousands, demand only that their governments seriously try to achieve arms control and disarmament, while maintaining a military balance with the Soviet Union. They took to the streets in favor of a freeze on nuclear weapons production, for example, as they became convinced that the West and in particular the Reagan administration had stopped trying. Activists and ordinary citizens could be kept apart if the administration presented itself as willing to try to negotiate arms reductions with the Soviet Union.

SDI, which the administration presented as a defensive rather than offensive system, was well suited to this approach. By espousing SDI, the president held out the hope of the complete elimination of nuclear weapons and their replacement by nonnuclear defenses. In this sense SDI is an exceptionally appealing demonstration of the peaceful intentions of the administration.

Reagan's View of the U.S. World Role

In addition to these strategic and political considerations, there were other reasons for the turn to SDI. President Reagan and his advisers' views of the U.S. world role and capabilities and of U.S.-Soviet relations differ strikingly from those of many policymakers in the Ford and Carter administrations. Three of the most important differences concern (1) the reassertion of U.S. global power, (2) U.S.-Soviet relations, and (3) the value of bilateral U.S.-Soviet agreements on strategic nuclear arms control.

From the outset Reagan and his advisers were determined to reassert U.S. power and influence on a global scale. This approach involved a worldview contrary to that forced on the Nixon administration by Congress and public opinion after Vietnam and adopted by President Carter—a worldview that minimized the importance of the direct exercise of U.S. power and wealth in shaping world affairs. The minimizing view became popular for many reasons, including the failure of U.S. policy in Vietnam and the concurrent fracturing of the domestic consensus on foreign policy (the "Vietnam syndrome"). In addition, nations in many parts of the world had become increasingly self-confident and resentful of U.S. direct intervention. In the late 1960s and throughout the 1970s U.S. policymakers and many observers and critics concluded that the Vietnam syndrome and international opposition restricted the capacity of the United States to play the kind of active world role that it had undertaken in the first decades after World War II.

The result was an increasingly passive and fundamentally reactive foreign policy that reached its nadir in the Ford and Carter years. From the rescue of Americans taken prisoner by the Pol Pot regime in Cambodia in 1975 until the fiasco in the Iranian desert during the Tehran hostage crisis in 1980, the United States sought to avoid bold foreign engagements and obligations. The strategy that informed U.S. national security policy was to take advantage of the intense rivalries and nationalisms at work around the world and to enhance U.S. security through an astute understanding and adroit manipulation of regional conflicts, such as that between the Soviet Union and China.

The Reagan administration, though not disavowing some aspects of this approach, was convinced that the United States needed to act more forcefully on the world scene, whether through covert aid to anticommunist guerrillas in Angola, Afghanistan, or Nicaragua, or through the overt employment of U.S. forces in Lebanon and Libya. As it moved against Soviet influence around the world, the Reagan administration also wished to use the comparatively greater wealth of the United States and the attractiveness of the market system against the Soviet Union. Although the Soviet and U.S. economic systems are fundamentally different, the burden of SDI, even of markedly increased expenditures on research and development much less deployment, would be felt much more heavily in the smaller and less efficient Soviet economy than in its larger U.S. counterpart.

The Reagan administration views of the U.S.-Soviet relationship are not widely shared among the policymakers and academic specialists who have shaped past U.S.-Soviet relations. Among the most striking differences are those over strategic arms control. The Reagan administration departs from the traditional U.S. arms control position by paying less attention to areas that are negotiable with the Soviet Union and according greater importance to arms control measures whose acceptance would work markedly to the advantage of the United States.

The original Reagan administration proposal to cut the number of strategic warheads on each side to 5,000 is perhaps the best example of the new approach. A cut of this scope could not be made without seriously reducing the Soviet capability to attack U.S. ICBMs with its land-based missiles. When it was presented in 1982, the proposal's critics attacked it because it was nonnegotiable. However, unlike President Carter, who made a stab at deep reductions and then retreated, President Reagan stuck to his plan. Even when the Soviet government walked out of the strategic and intermediate nuclear force reduction talks with the United States in 1983, vowing not to return until the United States withdrew its new intermediate-range missiles from Western Europe, the president and his advisers maintained their commitment to deep reductions. Their stand appeared to have been vindicated when the Soviet Union, politically outmaneuvered, returned to the arms control talks without having stopped the deployment of the U.S. missiles in Europe or having brought about a single significant change in the U.S. position. Subsequently, the new head of the Soviet Communist party, Mikhail Gorbachev, embraced the call for deep reductions, went to a summit meeting with President Reagan, and tried to outbid the president with his own far-reaching arms control proposals. The successful stand on European missiles and the resumption of arms control talks can only have confirmed the Reagan administration's belief in the advantages of its approach to negotiating with the Soviet Union.

A number of influential members of the administration believe that arms control limits the United States more than it restrains the Soviets, that unilateral actions rather than arms control must be the basis of U.S. security, and even that the era of complex negotiated arms control agreements is past. Assistant Secretary of Defense Richard Perle and strategist Edward Luttwak, among others, have concluded that the West is inherently at a disadvantage in arms control negotiations with the Soviet Union. In their view, the many policymakers in the West, including large numbers of legislators in the United States and Western Europe, accord enormous importance to arms control negotiations. To these, the urgency of reducing nuclear arsenals is a decisive argument against virtually any further increases in spending on offensive nuclear forces, which would undermine the mutual trust needed for success in the U.S.-Soviet arms reduction talks. Helped by the popularity of this view and immune to similar pressures, according to Perle and Luttwak, the Soviet government can work for the greatest possible concessions during arms control negotiations as it modernizes its nuclear arsenal, knowing that pro–arms control sentiment in the West will limit the ability of the U.S. government to modernize its nuclear forces and to bargain aggressively.

These considerations combined to make the president and his advisers dubious about arms control and determined not to allow arms control to be posed as an alternative to the strategic build-up they believed necessary to offset the Soviet gains of the 1970s. Inevitably this policy led to a downgrading of the importance of arms control and an increase in the urgency with which the administration sought to achieve unilateral strategic improvements. The possibility that SDI might disrupt arms control negotiations has much less significance for the Reagan administration than it would have had in the Carter, Ford, and Nixon administrations.

SDI AND STRATEGIC ARMS CONTROL

Arms control and SDI are inextricably linked; the Soviet government has repeatedly said that no progress can be made on arms control negotiations until the United States abandons SDI. Understandably, supporters and critics of SDI hold profoundly different estimates of SDI's effect on existing arms control agreements, such as the ABM Treaty and the two agreements to control offensive nuclear arsenals reached in the Strategic Arms Limitation Talks, SALT I and SALT II. What will be the Soviet reaction to SDI? Would the Soviets expand their offensive weapons to overwhelm SDI? Would they feel obliged to match the U.S. effort by building a strategic defense system of their own? Would all-out pursuit of SDI by either side destroy all hopes of limiting offensive nuclear arms? Is the administration's SDI program permissible within the terms of the ABM Treaty?

SDI's Potential Effect on Offensive Nuclear Arms

The Reagan administration argues that SDI can increase the willingness of both sides to agree to significant reductions in the numbers of offensive nuclear weapons and can enhance crisis stability, since neither side would have to fear the immediate loss of its deterrent forces. Even some outspoken critics agree that SDI would offer protection to citizens against a substantially reduced Soviet nuclear arsenal. The Reagan administration proposes to work for a "negotiated transition" from the present total reliance on offensive deterrence to a future marked by smaller offensive arsenals and an increasing role for defensive weapons. The administration's critics answer that SDI will aggravate the offensive arms race as each superpower mobilizes its resources to offset the defensive gains it fears the other may make.

The critics of SDI suggest that logically each superpower will increase and improve its offensive weaponry to counter innovations in defense. But Colin Gray and other supporters of SDI have just as logically argued that the Soviets will not necessarily launch a massive offensive build-up in response to SDI and will be willing to explore the "negotiated transition" proposed by the Reagan administration as a move from total reliance on offense to a mixed offensive-defensive reliance and ultimately to nonnuclear defenses alone. Logic will take us this far but no farther.

To date, the critics of SDI seem to have won this argument; they are able to go beyond logic and to point to two actions that support their skepticism. In the early 1960s the United States became aware that the Soviets had decided to deploy antimissile defenses, and in response it deployed multiple reentry vehicles (MRV) or warheads (the explosive part of a missile) on its submarine-launched ballistic missiles (SLBM). The addition of MRVs turned each missile into a shotgun with three warheads. Their deployment in submarines made them invulnerable to attack because the submarines could not be found before launching their missiles. The primary purpose of this offensive build-up was to overwhelm any defense and to maintain an assured-destruction capability against Soviet cities. Beginning in the early 1970s the number of warheads and their accuracy were increased through the deployment of multiple independently targetable reentry vehicles on U.S. ICBM and SLBM.

Since President Reagan's speech in March 1983, the Soviet government has taken the stand that the two countries can make no progress on arms control negotiations unless the United States abandons SDI. However, Soviet statements on this subject have not all been identical; there have been hints of the possibility of progress on reductions in the number of U.S. and Soviet nuclear missiles in Europe without an end to SDI. However, the apprehensions of the Soviet government are obvious. Their position is similar to that of the critics; they reject embarking on a negotiated transition. In their eyes SDI represents a U.S. drive to regain nuclear superiority, and they seem determined to respond with whatever combination of offensive and defensive measures is needed to counter SDI.

Prospects for a Successful Defensive System

In an effort to meet some of the criticisms of SDI, in early 1985 Special Presidential Adviser Paul Nitze advanced two criteria that would have to be satisfied before a decision for the deployment of a strategic defense system could be taken. To be deployable, SDI would have to be cost-effective at the margin—cost less to deploy than to counter—and safe against attack while it defended. The Nitze criteria were adopted as administration policy in National Security Decision Directive 172. The two standards no doubt were intended to reassure the Congress and to allow the president to keep the strongest supporters of SDI from overriding others in the administration and to be certain that progress on SDI did not needlessly harm relations with U.S. allies in Europe or the Soviet Union.

By May 1986 Nitze's criteria were attacked within the U.S. government. A Defense Department report to Congress on SDI omitted the "cost-effective" phrase altogether and stressed that the term signified much more than mere economics. Officials at the Pentagon argued that a strategic defensive system could become so important to the security of the country that it ought to be deployed even if it were more expensive than Soviet countermeasures. Moreover, the head of the SDI research program, General James Abrahamson, had begun to use the term "affordability"—a much more permissive standard.

The report and General Abrahamson's elastic terminology are symptoms of much more severe and important disagreements over SDI within the Reagan administration and particularly between the Defense and State departments. They disagree about the prospects of building a successful defensive system: Defense is optimistic, State pessimistic. More important, they differ about the extent to which the ABM Treaty should and does restrain the development of SDI. As a result of the disagreement, the terms of the ABM Treaty have become the subject of intense controversy.

Reinterpretation of ABM Treaty

The first important signs of SDI's impact on the ABM Treaty became publicly known in October 1985. In statements to reporters Assistant Secretary Perle and the president's National Security Adviser, Robert McFarlane, confirmed that they believed the United States could conduct research, development, and testing of SDI as if the ABM Treaty did not exist. Assistant Secretary Perle told reporters, "We have the legal right under the treaty to conduct research and development and testing unlimited by the terms of treaty." For several days it appeared that the Reagan administration had reinterpreted the sections of the treaty pertaining to the development and testing of defensive weapons based on new technologies.

The new interpretation was immediately challenged by several people who had negotiated the ABM Treaty, by arms control specialists, and by Secretary of State George Shultz. The disagreement centered on two provisions of the ABM Treaty. In Article V(1), the United States and the Soviet Union agreed "not to develop, test, or deploy ABM systems or components which are sea-based, air-based, space-based, or mobile land-based." In other words, only fixed land-based defenses are allowed by the treaty. The second provision, Agreed Statement D, covers technologies that were not in existence in 1972 when the treaty was signed: "In the event ABM systems based on other physical principles and including components capable of substituting for ABM interceptor missiles, ABM launchers, or ABM radars are created in the future, specific limitations on such systems and their components would be subject to discussion . . . and agreement."

These two statements could be read broadly in a way that would put SDI altogether outside the ABM Treaty. The legal adviser to the State Department, Abraham Sofaer, told the House Foreign Affairs Committee in October 1985 that this interpretation could be made by maintaining that the reference to "ABM systems and components" in Article V(1) pertains to those known to the parties in 1972. Only missiles, launchers, and radars are given in the treaty as parts of ABM systems. According to this view the quite different and new components of SDI systems—the lasers, rail guns, and particle beams—would not be subject to the limits of the ABM Treaty.

The claim was immediately and bitterly denied by some of the principal architects of the treaty, including Gerard Smith, former head of the Arms Control and Disarmament Agency and chief SALT negotiator in the Nixon administration. Smith and others insisted that the broad interpretation ignored the negotiating history of ABM and the intent and spirit of the treaty. They argued that the treaty had a narrow aim: to ban all nationwide defense systems of any kind. The treaty allowed only land-based fixed defenses and subjected those to stringent limitations in area and numbers. Alton Frye, an arms control specialist at the Council on Foreign Relations, argued that the legislative history of the treaty supported the narrow interpretation of its provisions. During hearings on the treaty, Senator Henry Jackson had criticized the limits it placed on developing new technologies. Frye added that at least one conservative, Senator James Buckley, had voted against the treaty because it prohibited the development and testing of lasers for military uses in space.

Under attack in and out of Congress, the administration retreated from the broad reading of the ABM Treaty and took refuge in a legalistic compromise. This reaction seemed to indicate that the administration was divided between those indifferent to the maintenance of the treaty and the consequences of a breach and those who feared the domestic and international political consequences. The compromise held out half a loaf to both the "broad" and "narrow" positions.

As Nitze told the House Foreign Affairs Committee in October 1985:

It is our view, based on our recent analysis of the treaty text and all of the accompanying records, that a broader interpretation of our authority than that which we have applied to restrict our SDI research program is fully justified. This is, however, a moot point. Our SDI research program has been structured and, for solid reasons, will continue to be conducted in accordance with a restrictive interpretation of the treaty's obligations. (Current Policy No. 755, October 1985)

The sense of the compromise seemed clear. There was no need to break or appear to be breaking the ABM Treaty in the immediate future. It will be some years before SDI components can be developed whose testing would violate the ABM Treaty.

FINAL OBSERVATIONS

If not a majority, at least a plurality of outstanding U.S. scientists, such as Nobel laureate physicists, oppose SDI on the grounds that it is technically impossible to achieve. They also oppose SDI because they believe that the Soviet Union would aggressively attempt to defeat it by various measures, possibly including a huge offensive build-up. This is as much a political as a technical judgment. The scientists who support SDI do not guarantee that it will work; rather, they insist that the chances of success are sufficient to justify mounting a very aggressive and expensive research and development program to find out whether SDI is technically feasible.

There are dangers in opening the question of strategic defense as the administration has done. The two superpowers may stumble into what theoretical physicist Freeman Dyson called "technical follies"—the production of defensive weapons systems that consume vast amounts of resources and point only to terror and loss rather than survival. This could be the result if SDI triggers either a defensive or an offensive-defensive arms race.

On the other hand, if the United States and the Soviet Union agree to work toward a negotiated transition, during which offensive arsenals would be drastically cut and defensive systems introduced to protect the remaining few hundred offensive missiles on each side, SDI would have played a role as a catalyst in major nuclear arms reductions. This transition could lead to a defense-dominated future, one in which, as Dyson described it, the stockpile of nuclear arms on earth is reduced through negotiations and the reductions are stabilized and ensured by defensive systems.

Opponents of SDI fear that it will ignite a new round in the nuclear · arms race. They urge a return to the steady, unspectacular process of bilateral strategic arms control negotiations. SDI's supporters counter that this approach grants the Soviet Union a strategic and political advantage, one that can be denied through an adroit linkage of offensive and defensive measures.

Is SDI for trading or building? Here is the most tantalizing question of all. Presidential Adviser Nitze has openly said SDI is for trading. His stance has been rejected by Secretary of Defense Weinberger and others at the Defense Department, who publicly maintain their commitment to deployment at the earliest feasible moment.

At this writing, there have been several intriguing developments. Despite President Reagan's announcement on May 27, 1986, that the United States would no longer be bound by the terms of the unratified SALT II agreement, the Soviet government on May 29 proposed deep reductions in offensive nuclear missiles in exchange for stringent limits on SDI, to be accomplished by a 15- to 20-year extension of the ABM Treaty. In a press conference in Washington on June 23, 1986, President Reagan appeared to welcome this approach. The president explicitly accepted the principle of major reductions. He was then asked if he could accept the Soviet insistence on linking reductions to restraint of SDI deployment. In his answer Reagan hinted strongly that the United States would insist only on a free hand to conduct research and would consider limits on deployment of SDI in exchange for major offensive reductions.

The basis of a new U.S.-Soviet arms control agreement would be to allow research on SDI and to postpone deployment (which will not be feasible for years except for the defense of silos) in exchange for major reductions in the number of offensive missiles on each side. The outcome of the agreement remains very uncertain. It may prove impossible for one or both sides to agree to the offensive reductions. Reagan administration policymakers may be unable to reach accord among themselves about the terms of an SDI-offensive bargain. The Soviets may renege. Most of the important decisions about SDI will be made after the Reagan administration leaves office in 1989, and a successor administration quite possibly may take a different approach to SDI. Even so, the new U.S.-Soviet initiatives are encouraging and suggest that it may be possible to reconcile the positions of the critics and supporters of the SDI through a new U.S.-Soviet arms control agreement.

The following readings present the major arguments for and against the Strategic Defense Initiative and representative opinions regarding its strategic and technical feasibility and its possible effects on U.S.-Soviet and U.S.-allied relations. Taken together they address the central political and technical questions about strategic defense. Is SDI a pipe dream or a revolutionary and potentially beneficial approach to the nuclear dilemma? Is SDI technically feasible or is it beyond the capabilities of near-term or long-term technological development? Will the repercussions of SDI be a Soviet build-up or will it serve as a catalyst for bilateral arms reductions? In particular, is SDI intended primarily to outrun the Soviets technically and to strain their economy? Or should SDI be used as a bargaining chip? For what should it be exchanged? Will SDI lead to stable and predictable relations between the superpowers? Should the United States pursue SDI if a cooperative negotiated transition fails to develop? What adjustments in SDI are necessary to maintain bipartisan domestic support in the United States and the cooperation of the nation's Western European allies?

Bibliography: Introduction

Boutwell, Jeffrey, and Scribner, Richard A. *The Strategic Defense Initiative: Some Arms Control Implications.* Washington, D.C.: American Association for the Advancement of Science, 1985.

Carter, Ashton B., and Schwartz, David N., eds. *Ballistic Missile Defense.* Washington, D.C.: Brookings, 1984.

Dam, Kenneth W. "Geneva and Beyond: New Arms Control Negotiations," address before the Foreign Policy Association, New York, January 14, 1985. Reprinted in U.S. State Department, Bureau of Public Affairs, Current Policy No. 647, January 1985, pp. 1–3.

Durch, William J., ed. *National Interests and the Military Use of Space.* Cambridge: Ballinger, 1984.

Graham, (General) Daniel. *High Frontier.* New York: Tom Doherty Associates, 1983.

Jastrow, Robert. *How to Make Nuclear Weapons Obsolete.* Boston: Little, Brown, 1983.

Journal of International Affairs. Summer 1985.

Karas, Thomas. *The New High Ground: Systems and Weapons of Space Age War.* New York: Simon and Schuster, 1983.

Long, Franklin A., Hafner, Donald, and Boutwell, Jeffrey, eds. *Weapons in Space.* New York: Norton, 1986.

Nitze, Paul H. "Negotiations on Nuclear and Space Arms," address before the Foreign Service Institute Symposium on "The Future of Start," Arlington, Virginia, March 13, 1986. Reprinted in U.S. State Department, Bureau of Public Affairs, Current Policy No. 807, March 1986, pp. 1–4.

———. "U.S. Strategic Force Structures: The Challenge Ahead," address before the American Institute of Aeronautics and Astronautics Strategic Systems Conference, Monterey, California, February 4, 1986. Reprinted in U.S. State Department, Bureau of Public Affairs, Current Policy No. 794, February 1986, pp. 1–4.

———. Statement before the Subcommittee on Arms Control, International Security, and Science of the House Foreign Affairs Committee, Washington, D.C., October 22, 1985. U.S. State Department, Bureau of Public Affairs, Current Policy No. 755, October 1985.

Payne, Keith B. *Strategic Defense: 'Star Wars' in Perspective.* Lanham, Md.: Hamilton Press, 1986.

U.S. Congress, Office of Technology Assessment. *Ballistic Missile Defense Technologies.* Washington, D.C.: Government Printing Office, 1985.

Weinberger, Caspar W. "What is Our Defense Strategy?" News Release, Office of the Assistant Secretary of Defense, October 9, 1985.

PART ONE

THE REAGAN STRATEGIC DEFENSE INITIATIVE

President Reagan in his speech of March 23, 1983, set forth the goal of rendering nuclear weapons "impotent" and "obsolete." The president challenged the scientific community to create a defense system that embodied the newest technologies that could protect the entire U.S. population from attack by nuclear ballistic missiles.

After the speech two U.S. government study teams were established: A team led by Fred Hoffman reported on the strategic feasibility of defense; a second group led by James Fletcher examined technical feasibility. The Hoffman team advised that defense, even one limited to protection of hard sites—missile silos and command centers—was strategically desirable. In particular the Hoffman group stressed the feasibility of pursuing interim measures, such as defense against tactical missile attack in areas such as NATO Europe.

The Fletcher committee concluded that great technical progress had been made since the signing of the ABM Treaty in 1972. The progress was so great that defense against ballistic missile attack might be possible. The Fletcher group proposed that the government initiate a major research effort to explore the prospects of developing and deploying a multilayer defense system. Missiles would be attacked during the first minutes of flight, or boost-phase, and at three or more other stages in flight toward the United States. If each layer was 80 percent effective, the cumulative defensive success rate would allow only 0.16 percent of the attacking missiles to reach their targets.

With these favorable reports in hand, the administration established the Strategic Defense Initiative Organization (SDIO) to administer the program described in General James Abrahamson's testimony. SDIO envisions the expenditure of $26 billion on research during the next five years.

According to General Abrahamson SDI would develop in three stages. The research phase would last into the early 1990s. During this time the technical feasibility of SDI would be determined and the most promising approaches identified. Assuming a technically feasible approach is found, the second stage would be the shift from total reliance on offensive nuclear deterrence to substantial reliance on defense. This change would be accompanied by arms control negotiations and the effort to agree on substantial reductions in the numbers of nuclear weapons held by the Soviet Union and the United States. In the final phase the two superpowers would agree to reduce offensive nuclear arsenals to zero.

The criteria proposed by Paul Nitze would have to be met before a transition from offensive to defensive reliance could be made. According to Nitze, no defensive deployments should be made unless the system is cost-effective at the margin—cheaper to build than to counter—and invulnerable to attack. Nitze has added that a negotiated transition is essential, to prevent one side from either attaining a commanding lead or concluding that there would be an advantage in striking first.

CHAPTER 1

Address to the Nation on the Strategic Defense Initiative

Ronald Reagan

. . . My predecessors in the Oval Office have appeared before you on other occasions to describe the threat posed by Soviet power and have proposed steps to address that threat. But since the advent of nuclear weapons, those steps have been increasingly directed toward deterrence of aggression through the promise of retaliation.

This approach to stability through offensive threat has worked. We and our allies have succeeded in preventing nuclear war for more than three decades. In recent months, however, my advisers, including in particular the Joint Chiefs of Staff, have underscored the necessity to break out of a future that relies solely on offensive retaliation for our security.

Over the course of these discussions, I've become more and more deeply convinced that the human spirit must be capable of rising above dealing with other nations and human beings by threatening their existence. Feeling this way, I believe we must thoroughly examine every opportunity for reducing tensions and for introducing greater stability into the strategic calculus on both sides.

One of the most important contributions we can make is, of course, to lower the level of all arms, and particularly nuclear arms. We're engaged right now in several negotiations with the Soviet Union to bring about a mutual reduction of weapons. I will report to you a week from tomorrow my thoughts on that score. But let me just say, I'm totally committed to this course.

If the Soviet Union will join with us in our effort to achieve major arms reductions we will have succeeded in stabilizing the nuclear balance. Nevertheless, it will still be necessary to rely on the specter of retaliation, on mutual threat. And that's a sad commentary on the human condition. Wouldn't it be better to save lives than to avenge them? Are we not capable

---

Excerpted from March 23, 1983, "Address to the Nation on the Strategic Defense Initiative."

of demonstrating our peaceful intentions by applying all our abilities and our ingenuity to achieving a truly lasting stability? I think we are. Indeed we must.

After careful consultation with my advisers, including the Joint Chiefs of Staff, I believe there is a way. Let me share with you a vision of the future which offers hope. It is that we embark on a program to counter the awesome Soviet missile threat with measures that are defensive. Let us turn to the very strengths in technology that spawned our great industrial base and that have given us the quality of life we enjoy today.

What if free people could live secure in the knowledge that their security did not rest upon the threat of instant U.S. retaliation to deter a Soviet attack, that we could intercept and destroy strategic ballistic missiles before they reached our own soil or that of our allies?

I know this is a formidable, technical task, one that may not be accomplished before the end of the century. Yet, current technology has attained a level of sophistication where it's reasonable for us to begin this effort. It will take years, probably decades of efforts on many fronts. There will be failures and setbacks, just as there will be successes and breakthroughs. And as we proceed, we must remain constant in preserving the nuclear deterrent and maintaining a solid capability for flexible response. But isn't it worth every investment necessary to free the world from the threat of nuclear war? We know it is.

In the meantime, we will continue to pursue real reductions in nuclear arms, negotiating from a position of strength that can be ensured only by modernizing our strategic forces. At the same time, we must take steps to reduce the risk of a conventional military conflict escalating to nuclear war by improving our non-nuclear capabilities.

America does possess—now—the technologies to attain very significant improvements in the effectiveness of our conventional, non-nuclear forces. Proceeding boldly with these new technologies, we can significantly reduce any incentive that the Soviet Union may have to threaten attack against the United States or its allies.

As we pursue our goal of defensive technologies, we recognize that our allies rely upon our strategic offensive power to deter attacks against them. Their vital interests and ours are inextricably linked. Their safety and ours are one. And no change in technology can or will alter that reality. We must and shall continue to honor our commitments.

I clearly recognize that defensive systems have limitations and raise certain problems and ambiguities. If paired with offensive systems, they can be viewed as fostering an aggressive policy, and no one wants that. But with these considerations firmly in mind, I call upon the scientific community in our country, those who gave us nuclear weapons, to turn their great talents now to the cause of mankind and world peace, to give us the means of rendering these nuclear weapons impotent and obsolete.

Tonight, consistent with our obligations of the ABM treaty and recognizing the need for closer consultation with our allies, I'm taking an important first step. I am directing a comprehensive and intensive effort to define a long-term research and development program to begin to achieve our ultimate goal of eliminating the threat posed by strategic nuclear missiles. This could pave the way for arms control measures to eliminate the weapons themselves. We seek neither military superiority nor political advantage. Our only purpose—one all people share—is to search for ways to reduce the danger of nuclear war.

My fellow Americans, tonight we're launching an effort which holds the promise of changing the course of human history. There will be risks, and results take time. But I believe we can do it. As we cross this threshold, I ask for your prayers and your support. . . .

.

CHAPTER 2

Ballistic Missile Defenses and U.S. National Security

Fred S. Hoffman

President Reagan's directive to assess the role of defensive systems has required the Future Security Strategy Study to consider the relation of these systems to our strategic objectives and to Soviet programs and policy. The role of intermediate defensive systems has been a major focus of our study.[1]

THE NEED FOR DEFENSIVE SYSTEMS IN OUR SECURITY STRATEGY

There is a broad consensus that reliance on nuclear retaliatory threats raises serious political and moral problems, particularly in contingencies where the enemy use of force has been constrained. Technologies for defensive systems and those for extremely precise and discriminating attacks on strategic targets have been advancing very rapidly. (Many technologies are common to both functions.) Together they offer substantial promise of a basis for protecting our national security interests, and those of our allies, that is more humane and more prudent than sole reliance on threats of nuclear response. The case for increasing the emphasis on defensive programs in our national security strategy rests on several grounds, in addition to the broad, long-term objectives mentioned by the President in his March 23 speech:

• The massive increase in Soviet power at all levels of conflict is eroding confidence in the threat of U.S. nuclear response to Soviet attacks against our allies. A continuation of this erosion could ultimately undermine our traditional alliance structure.

Excerpted from the Summary Report prepared for the Future Security Strategy Study at the request of the Undersecretary of Defense for Policy. Fred S. Hoffman led the team of outside experts who prepared the report.

• If the Soviet Union persists in the buildup of nuclear offensive forces, for the next decade and beyond the United States may not wish to restore, by offensive means alone, a military balance consistent with our strategic needs. Soviet willingness and ability to match or over-match increases in U.S. nuclear forces suggest that while additions to our forces are needed to maintain the continued viability of our nuclear deterrent, such additions alone may not preserve confidence in our alliance guarantees.

• The public in the United States and other Western countries is increasingly anxious about the danger of nuclear war and the prospects for a supposedly unending nuclear arms race. Those expressing this anxiety, however, frequently ignore the fact that the U.S. nuclear stockpile has been declining, both in numbers and in megatons, while Soviet forces have increased massively in both. A U.S. counter to the Soviet buildup that emphasized increases in U.S. nuclear stockpiles would exacerbate public anxieties.

• Arms agreements, despite widespread Western hopes for them, have to date failed to prevent growing instability in the balance—and the deterioration—in the Western position relative to the East. Offensive force limitation agreements, originally associated in the U.S. arms control strategy with the ABM treaty, have failed to restrain the Soviet offensive buildup; de facto reductions in the explosive yield and size of U.S. strategy nuclear stocks have not prevented vast increases in the size and destructiveness of the Soviet stockpile.

• Rapidly advancing technologies offer new opportunities for active defense deployment against ballistic missile attack that did not exist when, over a decade ago, the United States abandoned plans for defense deployments against nuclear attack. Technologies for sensing and discrimination of targets, directing the means of intercept, and destroying targets have created the possibility of a system of layered defenses that would pose successive, independent barriers to penetrating missiles. There has been improvement in some (not all) aspects of defense vulnerability. Given successful outcomes to development programs and robustness in the face of Soviet counter-measures, such defenses would permit only a very small proportion of even a very large attacking ballistic missile force to reach target. Such defenses might also offer high leverage in competing with offensive response.

BALLISTIC MISSILE DEFENSES IN THE SOVIET UNION

The Soviets maintain a high level of activity in programs relevant to defenses against nuclear attack including:

• Active programs for modernizing deployed air and ballistic missile defense systems which together give them the basis for a very rapid deployment of widespread ballistic missile defenses, if they decide to ignore ABM treaty obligations completely and openly.

• Large and diverse R&D [Research and Development] programs in areas of technology for advanced ballistic missile and air defense systems.

• A space launch capacity significantly greater than our own, if not as sophisticated.

A substantial Soviet lead in deployed defensive systems, superimposed on their growing offensive threat against our nuclear offensive forces, could destroy the stability of the strategic balance.

The decision to initiate widespread deployment of ballistic missile defenses does not rest with the United States alone. The common assumption that it does it completely unjustified. The Soviets give every appearance of preparing for such a deployment whenever they believe they will derive significant strategic advantage from doing so. Their activities include some that are questionable under the ABM treaty. Unless the public is aware and kept aware of Soviet activities in this area, the United States will probably be blamed for initiating "another round in the arms race." The state of U.S. preparedness to deploy capable defenses will be an important element in the Soviets' assessment of their own options. Active U.S. R&D programs on advanced defensive systems can assist in deterring a Soviet deployment designed to exploit an asymmetry in their favor.

ALTERNATIVE PATHS TO THE PRESIDENT'S OBJECTIVE

The path to the President's ultimate objective may be designed to go directly toward the ultimate objective of a full, multilayered system that offers nearly leakproof defenses against very large offensive forces. Under some conditions such a path might be an optimal use of limited R&D resources, concentrating first on those technologies that present the greatest difficulty and require the greatest lead times.

Alternatively, R&D programs might be designed to provide earlier options for the deployment of intermediate systems, based on technologies that can contribute to the ultimate objective, as such systems become technically feasible and offer useful capabilities. Such a path toward the President's ultimate goal might generate earlier funding demands to support deployment of intermediate systems and would require early treatment of some of the policy issues.

Also, at least one variant considered in our report, an (Anti-Tactical Missile) deployment for theaters of operations, could be undertaken without modification of the ABM treaty.

The principal benefits of an R&D path providing options for earlier, partial deployments are:

• Possibilities for an early contribution to improving the deteriorating military balance.

• Its explicit provision of a hedge against the risks inherent in a program where each of a large number of demanding technological goals must be met in order to realize any useful result at all.

• The likelihood that early deployments of parts of the ultimate system may also prove to be the most effective path to achieving such a system; early operational experience with some system elements can contribute useful feedback to the development process.

INTERMEDIATE DEFENSIVE SYSTEMS, SOVIET STRATEGY,
AND DETERRENCE

Fundamentally, the choice between the two paths depends on the utility of intermediate systems in meeting our national security objectives. In the discussion of ballistic missile defenses that preceded the U.S. proposal of the ABM treaty, opponents of such defenses argued that the utility of widespread defense deployments should be judged in terms of their ability to protect population from large attacks aimed primarily at urban-industrial areas. Because of the destructiveness of nuclear weapons, nearly leakproof defenses are required to provide a high level of protection for population against such attacks. Moreover, opponents at that time also divided our strategic objectives into two categories: deterrence of war and limiting damage if deterrence failed. They relegated defenses exclusively to the second objective and ignored the essential complementarity between the two objectives. Consequently, they assigned defenses no role in deterrence.

We have reexamined this issue, and we conclude that defenses of intermediate levels of capability can make critically important contributions to our national security objectives. In particular, they can reinforce or help maintain deterrence by denying the Soviets confidence in their ability to achieve the strategic objectives of their contemplated attacks as they assess a decision to go to war. By strengthening deterrence at various levels of conflict, defenses can also contribute valuable reassurance to our allies.

Deterrence rests on the Soviets' assessment of their political/military alternatives. This, in turn, depends on their objectives and style in planning for and using military force. It also depends on their estimates of the effectiveness of weapons and forces on both sides. Soviet assessments on these matters may differ sharply from our own. Specifically, the past behavior of the Soviets suggests they credit defensive systems with greater capability than we do. If true, this will increase the contribution of defensive systems to deterrence.

Because of the long lead times, assessment of the strategic role of defenses also requires very long-term projections about the nature of the Soviet state. While such projections cannot be made with confidence, there is no current basis for projecting a fundamental change in the Soviet attitude toward external relations. We consider below the possibility that appropriate management by the West of its long-term relations with the Soviets might induce a fundamental change. Desirable as this goal is, the most probable projection for the foreseeable future is that they will continue to set a high priority on their ability to control, subvert, or coerce other states as the basis for their foreign relations. In this case, military power will continue to play a major role for the Soviets, and many present elements of style in the application of that power can be expected to persist:

• Domination of the Eurasian periphery is a primary strategic objective. The Soviets' preferred mode in exploiting their military power is to apply it to deter, influence, coerce—in short, to control—other states, if possible without combat. But the ability to so apply this power depends on strength in actual combat.

• The Soviet objective in combat is victory, defined as survival of the Soviet state and military power (with as little damage as possible) and the imposition of the Soviet will on opponents. Soviet doctrine and practice contemplate limited war, viewed in terms of Soviet ability to impose limitations on opponents for Soviet strategic advantage.

• Soviet plans unite the roles of various elements of military forces in a coherent strategic architecture, embracing offense, defense, and combined arms in various theaters of operations. Destruction of an enemy is subordinate to the achievement of the goal of victory. The Soviets' concept for use of strategic offensive and defensive capability is, consequently, to deter attacks by U.S. intercontinental forces, to separate the United States from its allies in the Eurasian periphery, and to limit damage in the event that U.S. offensive forces are used against the Soviet Union.

• Uncertainty is a dominant factor in all combat, creating an unlimited demand for superiority in forces. Soviet planners seek ways to control uncertainty but, faced with uncertainty over which they cannot exercise a high degree of control, Soviet military action may be deterred. Uncertainties are particularly important in technically complex interactions between offense and defense.

Such a view of military force and its political applications may appear inconsistent with Soviet threats of inevitable apocalyptic destruction in the event of war at any level—but such threats are intended to play on the fears of the Western public. While very great destruction might in fact result from Soviet attacks, the discussion above suggests that the Soviets give priority to military targets. In the absence of defenses, their massive offensive forces make it possible for them to attack large numbers of targets, including urban-industrial targets as well as high-priority military targets.

Whether they would conduct such attacks from the outset or withhold attacks against urban-industrial targets to deter U.S. retaliation must be a matter of conjecture. In any case, intermediate levels of defense capability might deny them the ability to destroy with high confidence all of their high-priority targets and force them to concentrate their attack on such targets, diverting weapons that might otherwise be directed against cities. Moreover, if defenses can deny the Soviets confidence in achievement of their military attack objectives, this will strengthen deterrence of such attacks. Thus, to the extent that such attacks are necessary to overall Soviet plans, defenses can help deter lower levels of conflict.

THE MILITARY UTILITY OF INTERMEDIATE DEFENSIVE SYSTEMS

Defensive systems affect attack planning in a variety of ways, depending on the characteristics and effectiveness of the defenses, the objectives of the attack, and the responses of the defense and offense to the measures adopted by the other side.

Any defense system can be overcome by an attack large enough to exhaust the intercept capability of the defense. The size of attack against which the defense is designed is therefore one major characteristic of a defensive system. The cost of expanding the defense to deal with a given increase in the size and cost of the offense is a measure of the leverage of the defense. Another characteristic is its effectiveness—its probability of destroying an offensive missile.

If the defense has sufficiently high capacity, effectiveness, and leverage, it can of course essentially preclude attacks. Such defenses may result from the R&D programs pursuant to the President's goal, but it is more likely that the results will be more modest. Even a modest level of effectiveness—for example, a kill probability of 0.5 for each layer of a four-layer defense—yields an overall "leakage" rate of only about 6 percent for an attack size that does not exceed the total intercept capacity of the various layers. Such a leakage rate is, of course, sufficient to create catastrophic damage in an attack of, say, 5,000 reentry vehicles (RVs) aimed at cities. It would mean 300 RVs arriving at targets—sufficient to destroy a very large part of our urban structure and population even if distributed in a nonoptimal fashion from the point of view of the offense.

Against an extensive military target system, however, with an attack objective of destroying large fractions of specific target sets (such as critical C³I facilities) with high confidence, such a leakage rate would be totally inadequate for the offense. The more specific the attack objectives and the higher the confidence required by the offense, the greater the leverage exacted by the defense. For example, in the previous four-layer case, if the [offense] required a high-confidence penetration against a specific target, it would need to fire at least 30 RVs to a single target since the defense firing doctrine is unknown to the attacker. As these are expected-value calculations, an attacker would have to double or triple the above values to attain high confidence in killing a specific target. Clearly an attacking force of 5,000 RVs that could destroy a very large military target system in the absence of defenses would be totally inadequate to achieve high confidence of destruction of a large fraction of a defended target set amounting to hundreds of targets. Yet, this is precisely what is required to achieve the strategic objectives of a large-scale nuclear attack.

The situation is even more dramatic in the case of limited attacks on restricted target systems, intended to achieve a decisive strategic advantage while continuing to deter further escalation of the level of nuclear attack. Such attacks would be precluded entirely by defenses of the sort discussed, would deny the attacker's confidence in the outcome, or would require a level of force inconsistent with limiting the level of violence, while depleting the attacker's inventory available for other tasks.

Offense and defense have a rich menu of responses from which they can choose. These include fractionation of payload to increase the number of warheads for a given missile force, the use of decoys, and the use of preferential offense or defense tactics. The outcome of the contest is likely to be uncertain to both sides so long as the defense keeps pace with additions to offensive force size by expanding its intercept capacity and upgrading its critical subsystems. Uncertainty about the offense-defense engagement itself contributes to deterrence of attack by denying confidence in the attack outcome.

We have considered the effect of introducing defenses in hypothetical representative military situations, taking account of what we know of Soviet objectives and operational style in combat. In their doctrine, the Soviets stress operations designed to bring large-scale conflict to a quick and decisive end, at as low a level of violence as is consistent with achievement of Soviet strategic aims. To achieve this objective in a conflict involving NATO, a major aspect of their operations is intense initial attacks on critical NATO military targets in the rear, particularly those relevant to NATO's theater nuclear capabilities and air power. Such attacks (including those in the non-nuclear phase of combat) are intended to contribute to Soviet goals at that level, to reduce NATO's ability and resolve to initiate nuclear attacks if the non-nuclear defense fails to hold, and to assist in nuclear preemption of a NATO nuclear attack. High confidence in degrading NATO air power is also essential to support utilization of Soviet operational maneuver groups designed to disrupt NATO rear areas.

The Soviets plan to use a wide variety of means to accomplish this task. Tactical ballistic missiles (TBMs) are taking an increasing role in this mission during the initial stages of either nuclear or non-nuclear combat as their accuracy increases and the sophistication of high-explosive warheads increases. Inability to destroy critical target systems would cast doubt on the feasibility of the entire Soviet attack plan, and so contribute to deterrence of theater combat, nuclear or non-nuclear.

In the event of imminent or actual large-scale conflict in Europe, another high-priority Soviet task would be to prevent quick reinforcement and resupply from the United States. Early and obvious success in this respect, by demonstrating the hopelessness of resistance, might abort European resistance altogether or end a conflict in its very early stages. In the absence of defenses, the Soviets might attempt this task by non-nuclear tactical ballistic missile attacks on reception facilities in Europe. The Soviets could also accomplish this task with higher confidence by means of quite limited nuclear attacks on such facilities in Europe and on a restricted set of force projection targets in CONUS [Continental United States].

While the risk of provoking large-scale U.S. response to nuclear attacks on CONUS might be unacceptable to the Soviets, they might also feel that—given the stakes, the risks of escalation if conflict in Europe is prolonged, and the strength of their deterrent to U.S. initiation of a large-scale nuclear exchange—the relative risks might be acceptable if the attack size were small enough and their confidence of success sufficiently high. Without defenses, very small numbers of ballistic missiles could in fact achieve high confidence in such an attack. However, an intermediate ballistic missile defense deployment of moderate capabilities could force the Soviets to increase their attack size radically. This would reduce or eliminate the Soviets' confidence that they could achieve their attack objectives while controlling the risks of a large-scale nuclear exchange. The role of intermediate defenses in large-scale nuclear attacks has already been discussed at the beginning of this section.

Soviet response to prospective or actual defense deployments by the United States also will have longer-run aspects. The Soviets' initial reaction will be to assess the nature, effects, and likelihood of a U.S. defense deployment. Barring fundamental changes in their conception of their relations to other states and their security needs, they will seek to prevent such a deployment through manipulation of public opinion or negotiations over arms agreements. (We consider the possibility of a fundamental change in Soviet political/military objectives in the discussion of arms agreements below.)

If the Soviets fail to prevent the deployment of defenses, they will assess their alternative responses in the light of the strategic architecture discussed above, the effectiveness and leverage of the U.S. ballistic missile defenses, and other relevant U.S. offensive and defensive capabilities (e.g., air defense). If the new defensive technologies offer sufficient leverage against the offense and they cannot prevent the West from deploying defensive systems, the Soviets may accept a reduction in their long-range offensive threat against the West, which might be reflected in arms agreements. In this case, they would probably seek to compensate by increasing their relative strength in other areas of military capability. Their current program emphases suggest that they would be more likely to respond with a continuing buildup in their long-range offensive forces. However, such a buildup would not necessarily be sufficient to maintain their current level of confidence in the achievement of the strategic objectives of those forces.

MANAGING THE LONG-TERM COMPETITION WITH THE SOVIET UNION

Current Soviet policy on arms agreements is dominated by the Soviet Union's attempt to derive unilateral advantage from arms negotiations and agreements, by accepting only arrangements that permit continued Soviet increases in military strength while using the negotiation process to inhibit Western increases in military strength. There is no evidence that Soviet emphasis on competitive advantage over mutual benefit will change in the near future, unless a fundamental change occurs in the Soviet Union's underlying foreign policy objectives. Such a change might be induced in the long run by a conviction among Soviet leaders that the West was able and resolved to block the Soviet Union's attempts to extend its power and influence by reliance on military strength. If such a change occurred the possibilities for reaching much more substantial arms agreements might increase. In that event, it might also be possible to reach agreements restricting offensive forces so as to permit defensive systems to diminish the nuclear threat. Soviet belief in the seriousness of the U.S. resolve to deploy such defenses might itself contribute to such a change.

DEFENSES AND STABILITY

Deployment of defensive systems can increase stability, but to attain this we must design our offensive and defensive forces properly—and, especially, we must not allow them to be vulnerable. In combination with other measures, defenses can contribute to reducing the prelaunch vulnerability of our offensive forces. To increase stability, defenses must themselves avoid high vulnerability, must be robust in the face of enemy technical or tactical countermeasures, and must compete favorably in cost terms with expansion of the Soviet offensive force. A defense that was highly effective for an attack below some threshold but lost effectiveness very rapidly for larger attacks might decrease stability if superimposed on vulnerable offensive systems. Boost-phase and midcourse layers may present problems of both vulnerability and high sensitivity to attack size. Nevertheless, if this vulnerability can be limited through technical and tactical measures, these layers may constitute very useful elements of properly designed multilayered systems where their sensitivity is compensated by the capabilities of other system components.

A PERSPECTIVE ON COSTS

We do not yet have a basis for estimating the full cost of the necessary research program nor the cost of systems development or various possible defensive deployment options. It is clear, however, that costs and the tradeoffs they require would present important issues for defense policy. While not insignificant, total systems costs would be spread over many years. There is no reason at present to assume that the potential contributions of defensive systems to our security would not prove sufficient to warrant the costs of deploying the systems when we are in a better situation to assess their costs and benefits.

NOTES

1. The members of the Study Team were Mr. Fred S. Hoffman, Director; Mr. Leon Sloss, Deputy Director; Mr. Fritz Ermarth; Mr. Craig Hartsell; Mr. Frank Hoeber; Dr. Marvin King; Mr. Paul Kozemchak; Lt. Gen. C.J. LeVan, USA (Ret.); Dr. James J. Martin; Mr. Marc Millot; Mr. Lawrence O'Neill; and Dr. Harry Sauerwein. The work of the Study Team was reviewed by a Senior Policy Review Group consisting of Professor John Deutch; Dr. Charles Herzfeld; Mr. Andrew W. Marshall; Dr. Michael May; Professor Henry S. Rowen; General John Vogt, USAF (Ret.); Ambassador Seymour Weiss; Mr. Albert Wohlstetter; and Mr. James Woolsey. Supporting papers were contributed by Mr. Craig Hartsell, Dr. James J. Martin, Mr. John Baker, Lt. Gen. C.J. LeVan, Mr. Douglas Hart, Mr. Marc Millot, Dr. David S. Yost, Mr. Leon Sloss, and Mr. Frank Hoeber.

CHAPTER 3

On the Road to a More Stable Peace

Paul H. Nitze

* * *

THE STRATEGIC CONCEPT

In preparing for Secretary Shultz's January (1985) meeting with Foreign Minister Gromyko, we developed a strategic concept encompassing our view of how we would like to see the U.S.-Soviet strategic relationship evolve in the future. That concept provides the basis for our approach to next month's talks in Geneva. It can be summarized in four sentences.

During the next 10 years, the U.S. objective is a radical reduction in the power of existing and planned offensive nuclear arms, as well as the stabilization of the relationship between offensive and defensive nuclear arms, whether on earth or in space. We are even now looking forward to a period of transition to a more stable world, with greatly reduced levels of nuclear arms and an enhanced ability to deter war based upon an increasing contribution of non-nuclear defenses against offensive nuclear arms. This period of transition could lead to the eventual elimination of all nuclear arms, both offensive and defensive. A world free of nuclear arms is an ultimate objective to which we, the Soviet Union, and all other nations can agree.

It would be worthwhile to dwell on this concept in some detail. To begin with, it entails three time phases: the near term, a transition-phase, and an ultimate phase.

THE NEAR TERM

For the immediate future—at least the next 10 years—we will continue to base deterrence on the ultimate threat of nuclear retaliation. We have little choice; today's technology provides no alternative.

Excerpted from U.S. Department of State, Current Policy, No. 657, February 1985.

That being said, we will press for radical reductions in the number and power of strategic and intermediate range nuclear arms. Offensive nuclear arsenals on both sides are entirely too high and potentially destructive, particularly in the more destabilizing categories such as the large MIRVed [multiple independently-targetable reentry vehicles] Soviet ICBM [intercontinental ballistic missile] and SS-20 forces.

At the same time, we will seek to reverse the erosion that has occurred in the Anti-Ballistic Missile (ABM) Treaty regime—erosion that has resulted from Soviet actions over the last 10 years. These include the construction of a large phased-array radar near Krasnoyarsk in central Siberia in violation of the ABM Treaty's provisions regarding the location and orientation of ballistic missile early warning radars.

For the near term, we will be pursuing the SDI research program—in full compliance with the ABM Treaty, which permits such research. Likewise, we expect the Soviets will continue their investigation of the possibilities of new defensive technologies, as they have for many years.

We have offered to begin discussions in the upcoming Geneva talks with the Soviets as to how we might together make a transition to a more stable and reliable relationship based on an increasing mix of defensive systems.

THE TRANSITION PERIOD

Should new defensive technologies prove feasible, we would want at some future date to begin such a transition, during which we would place greater reliance on defensive systems for our protection and that of our allies.

The criteria by which we will judge the feasibility of such technologies will be demanding. The technologies must produce defensive systems that are survivable; if not, the defenses would themselves be tempting targets for a first strike. This would decrease rather than enhance stability.

New defensive systems must also be cost effective at the margin—that is, they must be cheap enough to add additional defensive capability so that the other side has no incentive to add additional offensive capability to overcome the defense. If this criterion is not met, the defensive systems could encourage a proliferation of countermeasures and additional offensive weapons to overcome deployed defenses instead of a redirection of effort from offense to defense.

As I said, these criteria are demanding. If the new technologies cannot meet these standards, we are not about to deploy them. In the event, we would have to continue to base deterrence on the ultimate threat of nuclear retaliation. However, we hope and have expectations that the scientific community can respond to the challenge.

We would see the transition period as a cooperative endeavor with the Soviets. Arms control would play a critical role. We would, for example, envisage continued reductions in offensive nuclear arms.

Concurrently, we would envisage the sides beginning to test, develop, and deploy survivable and cost-effective defenses at a measured pace, with particular emphasis on non-nuclear defenses. Deterrence would thus begin to rely more on a mix of offensive nuclear and defensive systems instead of on offensive nuclear arms alone.

The transition would continue for some time—perhaps for decades. As the U.S. and Soviet strategic and intermediate-range nuclear arsenals declined significantly, we would need to negotiate reductions in other types of nuclear weapons and involve, in some manner, the other nuclear powers.

THE ULTIMATE PERIOD

Given the right technical and political conditions, we would hope to be able to continue the reduction of nuclear weapons down to zero.

The global elimination of nuclear weapons would be accompanied by widespread deployments of effective non-nuclear defenses. These defenses would provide assurance that, were one country to cheat—for example, by clandestinely building ICBMs or shorter range systems, such as SS-20s— it would not be able to achieve any exploitable military advantage. To overcome the deployed defenses, cheating would have to be on such a large scale that there would be sufficient notice so that countermeasures could be taken.

Were we to reach the ultimate phase, deterrence would be based on the ability of the defense to deny success to a potential aggressor's attack. The strategic relationship could then be characterized as one of mutual assured security.

COMMENTS

Having thus outlined our strategic concept, let me offer some comments and perhaps anticipate some of your questions.

First, the concept is wholly consistent with deterrence. In both the transition and ultimate phases, deterrence would continue to provide the basis for the U.S.-Soviet strategic relationship.

Deterrence requires that a potential opponent be convinced that the risks and costs of aggression far outweigh the gains he might hope to achieve. The popular discussion of deterrence has focused almost entirely on one element—that is, posing to an aggressor high potential costs through the ultimate threat of nuclear retaliation.

But deterrence can also function if one has the ability, through defense and other military means, to deny the attacker the gains he might otherwise have hoped to realize. Our intent is to shift the deterrent balance from one which is based primarily on the ultimate threat of devastating nuclear retaliation to one in which non-nuclear defenses play a greater and greater role. We believe the latter provides a far sounder basis for a stable and reliable strategic relationship.

My second comment is that we recognize that the transition period—if defensive technologies prove feasible and we decide to move in that direction—

could be tricky. We would have to avoid a mix of offensive and defensive systems that, in a crisis, would give one side or the other incentives to strike first. That is precisely why we would seek to make the transition a cooperative endeavor with the Soviets and have offered, even now, to begin talking with them about the issues that would have to be dealt with in such a transition.

My third comment is that we realize that a world from which nuclear weapons have been eliminated would still present major risks. The technique of making nuclear weapons is well known; that knowledge cannot be excised. The danger of breakout or cheating would continue. Moreover, there would also be the potential problem of suitcase nuclear bombs and the like.

But even if all risks cannot be eliminated, they can be greatly reduced. Nothing is wholly risk free; one must compare the alternatives. It seems to me that the risks posed by cheating or suitcase bombs in a world from which nuclear arms had been eliminated from military arsenals would be orders of magnitude less than the risks and potential costs posed by a possible breakdown in the present deterrence regime based upon the ultimate threat of massive nuclear retaliation.

THE GENEVA TALKS

U.S. and Soviet delegations will meet in Geneva in roughly 3 weeks' time to begin negotiations on nuclear and space arms. In those talks, we will advance positions consistent with and designed to further the concept I have outlined.

At the end of January, I was asked by the press whether I was confident about the outcome of the upcoming talks. I replied that I was more confident than previously—that is, before the Geneva meeting between Mr. Shultz and Mr. Gromyko—but I still wasn't very confident. We must bear in mind that there are profound differences of approach between the two sides.

In Geneva, Mr. Gromyko stated the Soviet position clearly and unambiguously. It has, since then, been repeated by many Soviet commentators. The Soviets insist on the "nonmilitarization" of space; by that, they mean a ban on all arms in space that are designed to attack objects in space or on earth and all systems on earth that are designed to attack objects in space. They have expressed opposition to research efforts into such systems, in spite of their own sizable efforts in this field, which include the only currently operational ABM and antisatellite systems.

As to offensive arms reductions, the Soviets have yet to acknowledge the legitimacy of our concern about the threat we see in their large, highly MIRVed ICBM force. They continue to demand compensation for British and French nuclear forces and assert that U.S. Pershing II and ground-launched cruise missiles somehow represent a more odious threat than that posed to NATO Europe by the hundreds of SS-20 missiles now deployed.

In addition, the Soviets maintain that the three subject areas—strategic nuclear, intermediate-range nuclear, and defense and space arms—must not only be discussed in their interrelationship, but that it is not possible to implement an agreement in one area without agreement in the others. We believe otherwise; if the sides come to agreement in one area, we see no sense in a self-denying rule that would prevent the sides from implementing an agreement that would serve the interests of both.

There are obvious differences. We will present our views and listen carefully to Soviet proposals. We do not expect the Soviets to accept immediately our viewpoint or our concept as to how the future strategic relationship should evolve. The negotiators have their work cut out for them; the process will be complex and could well be lengthy. But with persistence, patience, and constructive ideas, we hope that Soviets will come to see the merits of our position—that it will serve their national interests as well as ours.

CONCLUSION

At the beginning of my remarks, I noted that the elimination of nuclear weapons has often seemed an impractical goal, one which has received little more than lip service. As you can see, the United States is going beyond that; the President has initiated a serious effort to see how it can be accomplished.

We do not underestimate the difficulties in reaching that objective. Quite frankly, it may prove impossible to obtain; and, even if we do eventually reach it, it will not be for many, many years—perhaps well into the next century.

But we cannot be anything but uneasy about the current situation, in which the nuclear arsenals of the world total tens of thousands of nuclear weapons. We owe it to our children, our grandchildren, and—in my case—to my great-grandchild to hold out for and to work toward some brighter vision for the future.

CHAPTER 4

Statement to Congress

Lt. General James A. Abrahamson

. . . I believe it is helpful to describe the goals of the program in terms of a notional schedule for a postulated move to a future strategy which includes defense. For example, we might describe such a defense evolution from today's sole dependence for deterrence on nuclear retaliation in the following notional steps:

A. *The Research Phase*: the period of time from the President's 23 March 1983 speech to the early 1990s when a decision on whether to enter systems development could be made by the President and Congress.
B. *The Systems Development (or full scale engineering development) Phase*: assuming a decision to go ahead, the period of time beginning in the early 1990s when prototypes of actual defensive system components are designed, built, and tested.
C. *The Transition Phase*: the period of incremental, sequential deployment of defensive systems. It is our intention that each added increment, in conjunction with effective and survivable offensive systems, would increase deterrence and reduce the risk of nuclear war. During this period, as the US and Soviet Union deploy defenses against ballistic missiles that progressively reduce the value of such missiles, significant reductions in nuclear ballistic missiles would be negotiated and implemented.
D. *The Final Phase*: the period of time during which deployments of highly effective multiphased defensive systems are completed and during which ballistic missile force levels reach their negotiated nadir. This is the goal expressed in the President's 23 March 1983 speech. If similar technical progress in defense against other means of nuclear attack has been attained by this time, such defenses could also be incorporated. The most difficult nuclear weapon to defend against is the ballistic missile; hence, defense against it is the specific objective of the programs collected under the SDI label. . . .

Reprinted from *Survival*, March-April 1985 (London: International Institute for Strategic Studies, 1985). This article was taken from a May 9, 1984, prepared statement by Lt. General Abrahamson to the Subcommittee on Defense of the U.S. House Appropriations Committee.

FUNDING

We plan an aggressive, adequately funded program to pursue the relevant technologies at the maximum reasonable rate. For Fiscal Year 1985 we are requesting approximately two thousand million dollars (total for DOD and DOE). We anticipate that during the Fiscal Year 1986–89 period, approximately 24 thousand million dollars will be required.

The program is not a 'new start' in the usual sense. Substantially all of the relevant technologies have been funded in previous years, but not all have been specifically related to defending against ballistic missiles. To implement the President's Strategic Defense Initiative, we have focused these previously existing related research efforts into a single program, and augmented the previously planned level of DOD funding for Fiscal Year 1985, 1,527 million dollars, by 250 million dollars, for a total request of 1,777 million dollars. The DOD request is for 71 per cent real growth in relevant technologies from Fiscal Year 84 to 85, and 16 percent relative to pre-SDI plans for Fiscal Year 1985. Part of the initiative includes technologies involving nuclear devices, which are developed by the Department of Energy. Their work in direct support of this initiative in Fiscal Year 1985 is a portion of their nuclear research, development and test funding. It is estimated at 210 million dollars (it is not a separate, specific line item) for a total program of two thousand million dollars.

The DOD portion of the program has been divided into five technical areas, and a new program element has been established for each of them. These program elements are:

1. Surveillance; acquisition, and tracking;
2. Directed energy weapons;
3. Kinetic energy weapons;
4. Systems analyses and battle management; and
5. Support programs.

THE CONCEPT OF DEFENSE

The flight of a ballistic missile can be considered in four phases. The first is the boost phase, in which the first and second stage rocket engines of the missile are burning. They produce an intense and unique infrared signature. In the second, or post boost phase, the bus separates from the main engines, and the multiple warheads are deployed from the bus, along with any penetration aids such as decoys and chaff. In the third, or midcourse phase, the multiple warheads and penetration aids travel on ballistic trajectories through space, above the earth's atmosphere. In the fourth, terminal phase, the warheads and penetration aids reenter the earth's atmosphere, where they are affected by atmospheric conditions.

Our program seeks to explore technologies enabling the engagement of attacking missiles in all four phases of their flight. This would require a number of capabilities, including global, full-time surveillance to warn of an attack. There is leverage in engaging the missiles in the boost phase, because the multiple warheads and penetration aids have not yet been deployed. After deployment, we must be able to discriminate warheads from decoys, so we can target only the real threats. We must be prepared for the attacking warheads to be salvage fused; therefore, our terminal defenses must engage them at as high an altitude as possible. And in addition to the individual engagement capabilities, we must have a survivable battle management system capable of efficient, global control.

The technologies for the terminal defenses are also likely to be applicable to defense against the shorter-range nuclear ballistic missiles, such as submarine-launched ballistic missiles and theater-range ballistic missiles, which may not have trajectories high enough to permit their attack with exoatmospheric systems, and which have short times-of-flight. Such technologies are important for defense of our allies.

THE TECHNOLOGIES

Surveillance, Acquisition, and Tracking

Surveillance, Acquisition, Tracking and Kill Assessment (SATKA) including sensing of information for initiation of the defense engagement and for battle management and assessment of the status of forces before and during a defense engagement against nuclear ballistic missiles. It also includes signal processing and data processing for discrimination of threatening reentry vehicles from other objects and backgrounds. A crucial philosophy of design is that surveillance and acquisition should be autonomous in each phase of the engagement, but that tracking and kill assessment should be consultative through battle management. These requirements are necessary so that the contributions to leakage from missed detections remain independent to insure very high quality tracking and kill assessment.

The goal of this program is to develop and demonstrate the capabilities needed to detect, track and discriminate objects in all phases of the ballistic missile trajectory. The technology developed under this program is quite complex, and any eventual system must operate reliably even in the presence of disturbances caused by nuclear weapons effects or direct enemy attack.

This program has several component technology development programs which culminate in hardware demonstrations. A focused effort to study the observables during each phase is the first major element of the program. Optical, infrared, and radar signatures of reentry vehicles and penetration aids will be measured. The new techniques of radar imaging represent another element. Similarly, optical imaging, using lasers rather than radar beams, will be pursued. Finally, a substantial effort is included to develop cooled infrared sensors and near real-time signal processing.

The technology programs outlined above will lead to a series of hardware demonstrations. Four key demonstrations have been identified at this time, with the possibility of more in the 1990s as technology progresses. One demonstration will be an advanced boost phase detection and tracking system. Another major demonstration is designed to track and discriminate attacking objects in mid-course using advanced Long Wavelength Infrared (LWIR) sensors. The ability of airborne infrared sensors to identify and track reentering objects will be demonstrated in the army's Airborne Optical Adjunct (AOA) development program. Ground radar imaging and tracking demonstrations will continue as part of the army's terminal and midcourse defense programs. As other technologies mature, such as radar and optical imaging, new demonstrations will be conducted. As these demonstrations are completed, we will have obtained the technical information required to decide whether defensive systems of the necessary capability can be built, considering this key element of the defense design.

DIRECTED ENERGY WEAPONS

This program pursues four basic concepts identified as potentially capable of meeting a responsive threat—space-based lasers, ground-based lasers, space-based particle beams, and nuclear driven directed energy weapons. It also provides for establishment of the National Tri-service Laser Test Range at White Sands Missile Range, New Mexico. The basic technical thrusts include beam generators (laser and particle accelerators), beam control, large optics, and acquisition, tracking and pointing. Our request includes funds to search for technological opportunities for new and innovative capabilities.

The goal of the Directed Energy Technology Program is to bring the most promising concepts for boost and post-boost phase intercept to an equivalent technical maturity in the early 1990s. At that point we expect to be able to demonstrate a readiness for technology validation in system level demonstrations of the concepts selected to move into that phase. To achieve that goal we plan to demonstrate the feasibility of the leading candidate beam generators by the mid 1980s and their scalability to weapon performance levels in the late 1980s or early 1990s. In beam control we will demonstrate by the end of the decade a capability to control wavefront errors, maintain beam alignment within the system, compensate for atmospheric effects, and provide the components necessary to transmit and control the high intensity beams. In large optics, we plan by the 1990s to demonstrate several approaches for providing the large diameter ground and space-based optics required for most directed energy concepts and all surveillance systems employing optical and electro-optical sensors. In our acquisition, tracking and pointing efforts, we envision in-space tests that verify our capability to point with the necessary precision, to acquire and track targets of interest, and to provide early experiments in imaging and designation. Finally, we are considering integrated technology experiments to show that we can integrate the weapon subsystems with requisite efficiency. With these demonstrations completed we will have provided the basis for a decision whether we are ready to move into the more complex system level demonstrations required in the technology validation phase of R&D.

Kinetic Energy Weapons

Kinetic energy weapons include interceptor missiles and hypervelocity gun systems. The primary roles for these weapons include (1) midcourse engagement of reentry vehicles not destroyed during boost or post boost phases, and of post boost vehicles that have not dispersed all of their RV, (2) terminal (i.e. endoatmospheric) engagement of RV not destroyed during the previous phases of their flight, (3) space platform defense against threats not vulnerable to directed energy weapons, and (4) boost-phase engagement of short time-of-flight, short range submarine launched ballistic missiles. Additional roles for these weapons include (1) boost phase intercept from space-based platforms, and (2) midcourse engagement from space-based platforms. The kinetic energy weapons will rely on nonnuclear kill mechanisms to destroy the intended target. The key technologies required to develop these weapons include (1) fire control, (2) guidance and control, (3) warheads and fusing for guided projectiles capable of being launched by missiles or hypervelocity guns, (4) hypervelocity launchers, and (5) high performance interceptor missiles.

The goals of the Kinetic Energy Weapons Program are: (1) expansion of the technology data base to support the development of improved and advanced weapons and (2) development and flight demonstration of kinetic energy weapons which are designed to satisfy the SDI mission needs outlined above. Technology programs are planned for endoatmospheric and exoatmospheric interceptor designs, a hypervelocity launcher design, and the systems engineering and analysis required to integrate the various advanced subsystems and components into effective system constructs. Investigations will also be undertaken in novel and advanced techniques which have the potential for a high payoff in performance and/or cost effectiveness in the design of these weapons systems. Hardware development and flight test demonstration of a number of kinetic energy weapons system designs will also be undertaken as part of this program.

System Analyses and Battle Management

This program has been divided into two technology projects. The Battle Management/Command, Control, and Communications Technology Project will develop the technologies necessary to allow eventual implementation of a highly responsive, ultra reliable, survivable endurable and cost effective BM/C^3 system for a low-leakage defense system. This BM/C^3 system is expected to be quite complex and must operate reliably even in the presence of disturbances caused by nuclear effects or direct enemy attacks. This program seeks to (1) develop the tools, methods, and components necessary for development of the BM/C^3 system, and (2) quantify the risk and cost of achieving such a BM/C^3 system to control the complex, multi-tiered SDI system. The systems analyses project will provide overall SDI systems guidance to weapons, sensors, C^3, and supporting technologies. Tasks include threat analyses, mission analyses, concept formulation, system conceptual design, and subsystem requirements definition, system evaluation, and technology assessment for all levels of a multi-tiered, low-leakage system.

One of our early tasks will be to conduct a 'sanity check' on the defense responsibilities allocated to the various phases of the multi-tiered system by the defensive technology study. Even though we know that many of our weapons and sensor concepts will require orders of magnitude performance improvements to accomplish the President's defense objectives, we also know that effective overall system guidance will efficiently focus these technology efforts and help us avoid 'gold plating' and 'blind alleys'.

Obviously, if such a defense system were deployed, it would require positive control of its operations. We have to be sure that we can turn the system on when it is needed and turn it off when it is not. Just as importantly, the system must not be regarded as a 'paper tiger' by the Soviets if it is to serve as an effective deterrent to nuclear war.

Therefore, its credibility must be based on a demonstrated capability to manage the surveillance, tracking and intercept actions over the multi-tiers of this complex system. The information processing capability, specifically the development of complex software packages, necessary to associate outputs from multiple sensors, performing discrimination and designation, and 'birth to death' tracking, plus kill assessment is expected to stress software development technology.

Our immediate need is for effective approaches and tools for achieving high performance processors and software, and responsive communications networks that provide high reliability and fault tolerance. Evaluation and demonstration of this complex defense system and its C^3 will largely depend upon simulation. Therefore, development of effective modeling and simulation tools will also be an early priority endeavor.

SUPPORT PROGRAMS

This program element funds a collection of essential efforts designed to provide timely answers to a variety of critical SDI support related questions. The defensive technologies study (the report of the Fletcher panel) identified two areas that should receive priority attention in the SDI program.

First, for each weapon concept under consideration, we must develop the ability to scientifically predict the minimum energy that will be required, in a variety of engagement scenarios, to kill unhardened, retrofit hardened, and responsively hardened Soviet systems. These data will have a large effect on our choice of candidate system concepts. The feasibility of SDI may well hinge on the results of these efforts. The lethality and target hardening project of the support programs effort is structured to provide these data.

Second, the ability of any deployed Ballistic Missile Defense system to survive in the face of dedicated attack and to continue to function effectively must be established. The concepts, technologies and tactics necessary to insure continued system effectiveness will be defined and developed under the survivability element of support programs. The output from this effort will be fed into all other elements of the SDI—particularly into the systems concepts and analyses efforts.

Additionally, support programs will fund development of the technologies necessary for improved space logistics capabilities. These include the advanced orbital transfer vehicle capabilities that SDI will likely require. We will also evaluate the technical feasibility and cost effectiveness of using extraterrestrial materials for certain SDI applications.

Many SDI system elements (weapons, sensors, etc.) will require large amounts of electrical power. The power and power conversion element of support programs will fund concept definition and technology development for multimegawatt power systems. This effort will fully exploit the technologies being developed in the joint NASA, DOE, DARPA SP-100 program. Both nuclear and nonnuclear systems and technologies will be considered.

THE DEPARTMENT OF ENERGY'S CONTRIBUTION TO THE SDI PROGRAM

Although funded separately, the DOE program is integral to the overall Strategic Defense Initiative program. DOE funded efforts include concepts for nuclear driven x-ray lasers, survivability and lethality, and support subsystems. Other efforts, such as space-based neutral particle beam technology, are being performed by the DOE laboratories with DOD funds. A memorandum of understanding, to be signed by the secretaries of defense and energy, is presently in coordination. It will establish specific relationships between the elements of DOD and DOE engaged in planning and execution of the SDI. In accord with current policy, the DOE will have primary responsibility for nuclear source development, and the DOD for applications, target acquisition, beam control, and pointing/tracking. The DOE laboratories have unique facilities and capabilities to address many aspects of these difficult problems. . . .

Bibliography: Part One

Abrahamson, Lt. General James A. Statement before the Senate Appropriations Committee, May 15, 1984.
———. Statement before the House Subcommittee on Economic Stabilization, December 10, 1985.
Cooper, Robert S. Statement before the Senate Armed Services Subcommittee on Strategic and Theater Nuclear Forces, May 2, 1983.
DeLauer, Richard D. Statement before the House Armed Services Subcommittee on Research and Development, March 1, 1984.
Department of Defense. Defense Against Ballistic Missiles: An Assessment of Technologies and Policy Implications. Washington, D.C.: Government Printing Office, April 1984.
Department of Defense. Report to the Congress on the Strategic Defense Initiative. Washington, D.C.: Government Printing Office, 1985.
Nitze, Paul H. "SDI: Its Nature and Rationale," address before the North Atlantic Assembly, San Francisco, California, October 15, 1985. Reprinted in U.S. State Department, Bureau of Public Affairs, Current Policy No. 751, October 1985, pp. 1–3.
"The President's Strategic Defense Initiative." White House pamphlet. Washington, D.C.: Government Printing Office, January 1985.
"Weapons in Space: The Controversy over 'Star Wars,'" a six-part series by Wayne Biddle, Philip M. Boffey, William J. Broad, Leslie H. Gelb, and Charles Mohr, New York Times, March 3–8, 1985.

PART TWO

STRATEGIC FEASIBILITY

Two main disagreements have arisen regarding the strategic feasibility of SDI; both concern the Soviet response. A number of influential policymakers and arms control advocates from previous administrations believe that the Soviet Union will greet SDI with a massive offensive nuclear build-up. Their point of view is captured in the title of the article by McGeorge Bundy, George Kennan, Robert McNamara, and Gerard Smith: "Star Wars or Arms Control."

Colin Gray, a strategist with deep reservations about the value of arms control agreements, argues the opposite view. Gray suggests that the response of the Soviet government is in no sense foreordained; instead, the Soviets will face a choice that is amenable to rational analysis. The outcome of the analysis will be affected by an assessment of the costs and benefits of entering with the United States on a negotiated transition or choosing to launch an offensive arms race, which the United States would be obliged to counter with its own build-up.

George Rathjens and Jack Ruina emphasize the second strategic problem. What will happen to strategic stability if one side, the United States, for example, begins to think it has acquired a reasonably effective defense against missile attack? Rathjens and Ruina are concerned that in a crisis the side with such a defense might believe it could strike first against the other's weapons and then successfully cope with the "ragged" retaliation from its enemy's damaged offensive forces. They doubt that even a reasonably effective defense can be built, but they are not confident that policymakers would accurately judge the capabilities of the defenses they had deployed.

George Keyworth, former science adviser to President Reagan, maintains that the United States must "play its technological trump" by developing and deploying major defensive systems. In his view, SDI will eliminate the risk of a disarming first strike and in this way enhance strategic stability. If the preemptive option is removed, Keyworth believes that SDI will provide strong and realistic incentives—perhaps the only realistic incentives— for both sides to make deep reductions in their nuclear arsenals.

CHAPTER 5

BMD and Strategic Instability

George Rathjens and Jack Ruina

. . . President Reagan's goal of a perfect defense stirred the interest of the general public and of many public figures who have long sought an alternative to deterrence based on mutual assured destruction (MAD). Yet MAD is not a policy capable of being changed by political will; it is rather the inevitable consequence of the superpowers having the nuclear arsenals they have. Recalling the Manhattan and Apollo projects, which overcame seemingly difficult technological problems, many argue in support of the president's initiative. They do so, however, not fully appreciating the difference between the SDI and these two earlier efforts, i.e., that the SDI involves competing against a determined and resourceful adversary *as well as* unlocking nature's secrets and harnessing technology.

A substantial amount of support for the SDI has also developed within the community of military technologists and strategists. This has occurred less from a belief that a perfect defense against nuclear weapons can be realized than from a general interest in defense missions far less demanding than that proposed by the president. The tension between the president's goal of a perfect defense and many of his supporters' more modest goals of limited defenses was reflected in the presidential study groups (especially the Fletcher and Hoffman panels) that were formed after the president's speech, as well as in the administration's January 1985 special SDI report.

More limited roles for BMD include those that were considered when BMD was a major national issue in the 1960s: minimizing damage in the event of an all-out ballistic missile attack; defense of hardened military installations such as ICBM silos and command-and-control facilities; defense against unauthorized or accidental attack; and defense against lesser nuclear powers. Additional justifications for BMD in the 1980s include limiting the possibility of a Soviet "light" attack with nuclear weapons, and inducing the Soviets to reduce their commitment to land-based missiles (now their

Excerpted by permission of the authors and *Daedalus,* Journal of the American Academy of Arts and Sciences, Weapons in Space, Vol. II: Implications for Security, Summer 1985, Cambridge, Massachusetts.

dominant nuclear force) in favor of other systems such as submarine-launched missiles (SLBMs), which to some seem less worrisome.

The counter-arguments to these more modest goals are also similar to those invoked in the past. The first argument is that BMD technology is not up to some of the tasks being considered. The second is that these objectives, if they need be met at all, can be better realized through means other than active defense. The third is that in reaction to U.S. BMD deployment, the Soviets will not only increase the size and capability of their offensive nuclear forces but will also develop and deploy a BMD system of their own that we must assume will be about as effective as ours. The result of this competition could be a net loss in the security of both countries. The fourth argument seeks to counter the claim that deploying a BMD of even limited capabilities would provide valuable operational experience for subsequent deployment of a system intended for population defense. Whatever fears a country might have about its adversary's "break-out" capability (rapid deployment of an operational system) would certainly be exacerbated by its development, training, production, and testing of a limited but operational BMD.

Concerns about deployment aside, the prospect of a greatly expanded SDI R&D program is troublesome. First, it will likely increase incentives for each side to improve its offense because of the enormous uncertainty in estimating the effectiveness of defenses during the R&D phase, and because of the inherent conservatism that leads military planners to base their R&D and procurement on worst-case analyses. In addition, the effect of the SDI program, and similar Soviet efforts, will be to undermine U.S.-Soviet arms-control negotiations, as neither side will be willing to make deep cuts in its offensive forces if work on strategic defenses is intensified. The reality of mutual assured destruction may be unsettling, but neither country is likely to give up, or even significantly reduce, its offensive retaliatory capability in the face of possible defensive deployments by the other. Indeed, the history of the nuclear weapons competition between the U.S. and the Soviet Union demonstrates that each country will do whatever it feels is necessary to maintain this capability for deterring nuclear attack.

We therefore see serious harm resulting from the current SDI program and similar Soviet BMD efforts. This includes:

1. an increase in U.S.-Soviet tensions and intensification of the arms race;
2. the possibility that one of the superpowers would withdraw from the ABM treaty and deploy some type of BMD, even one of doubtful effectiveness;
3. erosion of the confidence of our European allies who are deeply troubled by the implications an SDI program and possible BMD deployment might pose for their security;
4. a false sense that technology and new weapons systems can eliminate the threat of nuclear destruction.

We want to emphasize that we find the pursuit of strategic defenses worrisome for these reasons, and not—as some maintain—because of concern over *crisis instability*. In our view, fears that deployment of a (purportedly) effective population defense could lead to substantially increased risk-taking during a crisis, or possibly even to a preemptive first strike, on the grounds that such a defense would be more effective against a degraded retaliatory force, are unwarranted. The very possibility of such a defense, and its consequences for crisis instability, can be almost totally discounted given the offense-dominant nature of nuclear weapons, and the technical realities facing strategic defenses. . . .

COST-EXCHANGE RATIOS

One important consideration in judging the merits of any type of defensive system is the cost-exchange ratio involved, that is, the incremental cost to the offense to ensure the ability of its warheads to reach their targets, compared to the added cost to the defense to intercept those warheads.

As an illustration, consider whether it would make sense for the U.S. to invest in defense of its industry and population from nuclear attack using technology presently available. We can hypothesize a variety of defensive measures, including air defense, civil defense, and different BMD deployment schemes, that might save a million lives in the event of a nuclear attack, and then estimate the minimum cost to the Soviet Union of upgrading its offensive capabilities just enough to negate each of these hypothetical American investments.

If the Soviet Union could negate such defensive measures at a cost much lower than the incremental American investment in defense, then U.S. investment in defense would likely be of little use. Assuming the Soviet Union wanted to maintain its current ability to inflict damage on the U.S., it would presumably make whatever investment would be required to offset ours. If we, on the other hand, could develop a defense system that could be negated only by relatively costly Soviet improvements, investment by the U.S. in defense would seem desirable. In this case, the Soviet Union presumably would not react, because any improvement in its offensive capabilities could be negated by a much smaller American investment in defense.

There is a third possibility. If the cost-exchange ratio for the best defense option we could identify were near unity—if the marginal costs to the offense and defense were about equal—then deciding whether to implement the defense option would be more difficult. Would the Soviets be less or more determined to threaten additional destruction than we would be to negate that possibility? If both nations were to attach the same weight to that increment of destruction, could the U.S., with its stronger economy, more easily afford to reduce the expected damage than the Soviet Union could afford to offset that reduction?

In any event, estimates of cost-exchange ratios are of limited value since they generally reflect the likelihood that each country overestimates the effectiveness of the adversary's weapons programs, while underestimating his own. Nonetheless, ratios either highly favorable to the offense or highly favorable to the defense do indicate, respectively, offense and defense dominance. A ratio near unity may well imply a vigorous offense/defense arms race, with each side straining to offset the improvements made by the other. . . .

PERFECT DEFENSE

There is something unprecedented about a defense that would make nuclear weapons "impotent and obsolete": it *really would* have to be perfect, not just very good. Non-nuclear offensive systems have been "rendered impotent and obsolete" by defenses that were less than perfect (armored knights by archers and the musket, for example), but the challenge is much more difficult when the issue is defense against nuclear weapons, with their individual destructive power.

In non-nuclear combat, the survival of some percentage of the loser's military forces has rarely been militarily or politically important. But with defense against nuclear weapons there is a world of difference between 100 and even 99 percent effectiveness. The former would, indeed, make nuclear weapons "impotent and obsolete," except perhaps for coercive purposes against nations not having defenses. A defense that is 99 percent effective would, on the other hand, result in unacceptable leakage in a war between the superpowers. The detonation of even as few as five or ten Soviet warheads (less than one-tenth of one percent of the Soviet arsenal) on U.S. cities would cause unparalleled destruction, something McGeorge Bundy has rightly characterized as "a disaster beyond history."[1]

To relieve all public concern about nuclear weapons, to assure political leaders that a defensive system would eliminate the possibility of a nuclear explosion on their own or allied territory, and to convince one's adversaries that nuclear weapons would not be at all useful to them—and "impotent and obsolete" would have to entail all these things—a defense would have to be virtually 100 percent effective, and perceived as such by both sides. This means that the system would have to perform flawlessly the very first time it is called upon, that it be invulnerable to direct attack, and that it be effective against *all* means of nuclear weapons delivery, including aircraft and cruise missiles as well as ballistic missiles.

In summary, we do not believe perfect defense to be a realistic possibility, particularly if the Soviet Union reacts by improving its offensive capabilities, as the Hoffman panel has recognized is likely[2] (but as the manager of the SDI program does not).[3]

VERY GOOD—BUT LESS THAN PERFECT—DEFENSE

It is our conviction that even a very good defense is not a possibility, assuming one is dealing with a determined adversary with substantial resources at his disposal. By "very good," we mean a defense capable of affecting the behavior of nations in times of crisis. Defenses that would be 99 percent or more effective against a "first strike" would meet this criterion. Such defenses might well affect decisions by political leaders in the event of crises in the Middle East, the Persian Gulf, or Europe. [However] if one or both superpowers were confident that it could reduce the number of attacking warheads to a small number, say ten or less, then the U.S. and/or Soviet Union would presumably be willing to take larger risks in escalating a conflict. . . .

Such defenses would have a terribly—and we use this adverb literally—troublesome effect on crisis instability. However effective defenses in this range might be against an adversary's "first strike," they would be still more effective against a ragged retaliatory force.

Expected leakage could be sufficiently reduced to justify political/military decisions that would be judged unacceptable in the absence of defense. If technology and cost-effectiveness considerations warranted such defenses, a country might proceed with their development and deployment on the assumption that a situation might develop in which it would be willing to launch a first strike; once a defense system is deployed, the incentive to strike first in a crisis situation could be overwhelming. If an opponent's defenses were vulnerable, the attractiveness of preemption would increase. Country A might strike first at B's defenses, so degrading them that a significant number of A's warheads might then be delivered against B's offensive force, reducing it to the point where A's defenses could reduce the leakage from a retaliatory attack by B to "acceptable" levels. This creates quite an incentive, and a reciprocally reinforcing one, for both sides to strike first during a crisis.

We feel it necessary to stress again that, in our view, this type of very good defense is illusory, at least as it applies to confrontation between the superpowers. The ongoing competition between defensive developments on the one hand, and offensive countermeasures and defense suppression techniques on the other, will mean that even if some BMD systems are deployed, the goal of a perfect, or even very good, defense will be unattainable. For this reason, longer-term considerations of crisis instability should be of little real concern.

Concerns about arms-race instability, on the other hand, are indeed justified, inasmuch as arms races seem to be driven as much—or even more—by fear of what *might* happen as by what is likely. If there were even a remote prospect that either superpower, or both, could deploy defenses that would be 99 percent effective, there would be enormous pressure for the would-be defender to improve the figure and for its adversary to reduce it. From an arms-race perspective, it is difficult to imagine a prospect more destabilizing.

FAIR-TO-GOOD DEFENSES

Few advocates of the SDI, with the possible exception of President Reagan and Defense Secretary Weinberger, believe that perfect or very good defense, as we have used the term, is realizable. Some, however, do envisage the possibility of such dramatic improvements in defenses that the cost-exchange ratio may approach unity at, say, a 50 percent effectiveness level. That is, they envisage an offense-defense technological balance that would permit, if not lead to, the deployment of defenses and offensive forces such that the expected level of damage in the event of conflict would be around 50 percent, or anywhere in the range of 1–90 percent (our arguments are invariant over this range). Efforts to decrease the damage level to below 50 percent through additional increments of defense could be offset by incremental improvements in offenses at less cost, while efforts by the offense to increase the level of destruction beyond 50 percent could be negated less expensively by incremental improvements in defense.

Were technological developments to permit such defenses, we would expect to see strong interest in deployment, for if the cost-exchange ratio were unity at the 50 percent destruction level, it would surely be much more favorable to the defense at higher levels of expected destruction. Each side would presumably have an impetus to deploy defenses sufficient to hold damage to some level of destruction, perhaps 70 percent, that would clearly be cost effective, while its adversary would not be strongly inclined to try to increase it beyond that level. This would follow given the unfavorable cost-exchange ratio to the offense and the fact that it would gain little, if any, political-military utility from increments in prospective damage level in this range. . . .

OFFENSE DOMINANCE

We now turn to the current situation, in which the offense is dominant over virtually the whole range of destruction levels. This condition has obtained throughout the nuclear era, and is likely to persist between the superpowers for the indefinite future. As long as it does, we can be reasonably sure that the superpowers will invest the resources necessary to overcome each other's defenses. Since the 1950s, for example, the Soviets have spent billions of dollars upgrading their extensive air defense systems, yet the U.S. has continued its efforts to be able to penetrate them. Over the last decade, the U.S. has spent billions of dollars to modernize the B-52 bomber and equip it with short-range attack missiles and later with cruise missiles, to procure the advanced B-1 bomber, and to develop Stealth techniques that would allow U.S. bombers in the 1990s to evade radar detection and reach targets in the USSR. What makes this example particularly compelling is that, for both the U.S. and USSR, manned bombers are far less important for retaliatory deterrence than either ICBMs or SLBMs, yet the competition has continued. And, of course, there has been competition between ICBMs and ABMs, even though technology and cost-exchange considerations have always militated against large-scale defensive deployment, at least of a sort intended to protect cities and industry. ICBM penetration aids were developed in anticipation of the possibility of defenses being deployed, and the prospect of ABM deployments was also a—if not the—factor in the impetus to develop and deploy multiple warheads (MIRVs). Thus, almost every effort by one superpower to improve its defense capabilities can be expected to provoke improvement in its adversary's offense capabilities for as long as defensive developments do not significantly alter the current offense-dominated situation.

DEFENSE OF SELECTED MILITARY ASSETS

Up to now, we have been addressing defense of cities and populations, a fundamentally difficult problem, given the enormous destructive capability of nuclear weapons, the vulnerability of these targets, and the fact that loss of even a small fraction of them would be catastrophic. Defense of selected military targets, however (ICBM silos are usually cited), is a much easier task. It is quite possible that, unlike defense of population and social infrastructure, cost-exchange considerations will favor this type of defense. . . .

. . . The defense of military targets is often easier because it is possible to protect them against the effects of nuclear attack by passive means such as "hardening" (something not possible for cities), which enables them to survive near-misses. This is particularly important since the firing of defensive interceptors can be delayed until late enough in a warhead's trajectory for the defense to discriminate between warheads likely to destroy a target unless intercepted and decoys and warheads likely to miss their targets, or warheads aimed at targets already destroyed.

But cost-exchange considerations are not the only ones that bear on the decision whether to deploy defenses. One must also decide if the targets are worth defending, and whether there is indeed a threat. Placing a monetary value on the loss of a city and its population is clearly a formidable— some might argue, impossible—task; it is clearly easier to make judgments about the worth of missile silos or other military targets. One should also raise the question whether there are alternatives to defense that could accomplish the same military mission, e.g., providing for the delivery of a desired level of retaliatory attack. When such comparisons are made—and this must involve not just dollar costs, but considerations of stability and other factors—it could be that retaliatory deterrence would be better served by buying larger numbers of offensive missiles or by placing greater reliance on mobile systems.

However, in the absence of a considerably increased Soviet threat, we would argue against either buying defenses to protect U.S. strategic forces or increasing offensive forces. We would argue this on the grounds that the so-called "window of vulnerability" has been much overrated. As President Reagan's Commission on Strategic Forces, chaired by General Brent Scowcroft, recognized, the enormous uncertainties over whether a Soviet attack on U.S. strategic forces would be successful, and the tremendous risk that such an attack could lead to general nuclear war, make the threat of such an attack implausible, at least in the near term.

As a final note, we should point out that it is possible to develop and deploy a respectable terminal BMD system for hardened military targets with state-of-the-art technology. The Department of Defense has pursued relevant technologies for hard-target defense since the signing of the ABM treaty in 1972. Yet it is not at all clear that the massive SDI program now underway can or will lead to the development of hard-site defense systems that are any more useful or cost effective than those that might emerge from the continued orderly pursuit of BMD technology as it existed prior to the SDI. The SDI program therefore seems irrelevant to decisions about whether to pursue hard-site defense deployment; indeed, it may even be diversionary. . . .

POLITICAL EFFECTS OF THE SDI

. . . In all likelihood, a superpower competition in strategic defenses will lead to an increased Soviet-American offensive arms race. We expect that U.S. defensive developments will lead to an acceleration of Soviet efforts both to develop similar capabilities for defense and to improve offensive capabilities, and we can expect corresponding U.S. reactions to Soviet efforts. If this process continues for some time—and clearly, the SDI has a very distant time horizon—pressures will develop for some kind of BMD deployment in both countries. Indeed, support is already developing in this country for a defense of ICBM silos and other military assets. . . .

The most worrisome aspect of the SDI may finally be its political-psychological consequences. Our concern focuses primarily on four groups: the general American public, American elites, the leadership of countries allied with the U.S., and the Soviet leadership.

The immediate response to President Reagan's March 23 speech and subsequent information derived from polls indicate a great deal of resonance with the president's vision. Americans want their children, if not themselves, to look forward to a world without the threat of nuclear weapons; they find appealing the notion of a defense so effective as to render nuclear weapons impotent and obsolete. We, however, see this vision as diversionary and illusory; it deludes the public into thinking that the solution to the dual problem of nuclear weapons and a troublesome adversary can be resolved by new weapons systems, rather than by political means.

As we mentioned earlier, most of those in the technical community, and many others who are well informed and concerned about security matters, share our belief that a perfect, or even a very good, defense against a massive Soviet attack against U.S. population and industry is just not realizable. Yet, the president and his secretary of defense have continued to espouse the goal of a perfect defense not just against ballistic missiles, but against bombers and cruise missiles as well.

We are troubled that the SDI may raise special concerns in the case of Allied governments. They may well see the SDI and U.S.-Soviet competition in strategic defense as evidence of growing isolationism in the U.S., or as additional evidence that the U.S. is trying to deal with the Soviet problem mainly through military means, as opposed to political measures. There is also the fear that if limited American and Soviet defenses are deployed, both superpowers might be more willing to take increased risks in a crisis, which in turn could increase the vulnerability of Europe to a limited nuclear war. We discount this possibility, believing that there is no realistic prospect of defenses becoming that effective, nor even of their being perceived as that effective, but we cannot discount totally the impact of such beliefs in a time when actual deployment is a distant prospect. And there are those who hold that the prospect of a Soviet defense must call into question the effectiveness of British, French, and Chinese nuclear deterrents.

Finally, there is the Soviet reaction. The SDI must have raised questions in Moscow concerning the commitment of the U.S. government to the ABM treaty and current arms-control efforts. It must have reinforced the Soviet view that, despite the recent resumption of U.S.-Soviet arms-control talks, the Reagan administration is more interested in dealing with Soviet-American problems through military and technological competition than by political means. Indeed, because of Reagan's commitment to the SDI and statements by Secretary Weinberger to the effect that the ABM treaty should not stand in the way of strategic defense, the Soviet leadership must feel that the U.S. might trade off arms-control considerations in favor of military opportunities. In addition, there are probably at least some in the Kremlin who see the SDI as militarily threatening, as raising the possibility of first-strike capability.

In summary, we see virtually no chance of developing and deploying the perfect defenses that would be required to meet President Reagan's objective of "rendering nuclear weapons impotent and obsolete." We do not even see the possibility of deploying near-perfect ones. The president's public profession of his objective, as well as his and Secretary Weinberger's optimism about its realization, seem to us a triumph of wishful thinking and fantasy over reality: an act of surrender to the promise held out by technical fixes as the preferred means of dealing with nuclear arms and a difficult adversary—two situations that must ultimately be dealt with by political means.

The Strategic Defense Initiative stands out as the most bizarre episode in the sad history of the nuclear arms race. It is extraordinary that a U.S. president should include this theoretically laudable, but technically baseless, goal of negating nuclear weapons in his address to the nation; that he should continue to solicit support for the SDI as the centerpiece of U.S. strategic policy, both at home and abroad; that the community of ABM advocates has been reassembled and its goals legitimated; that technical experts who do not accept the unrealistic final goals of the SDI program have been able to include as intermediate goals a variety of partial defenses that require very different justifications from those put forth by the president; and that the suspension of good judgment has allowed the launch of an exploratory ABM program on a scale that is irreconcilable with both state-of-the-art technology and with reasonable pursuit of nuclear stability.

NOTES

1. McGeorge Bundy, "To Cap the Volcano," *Foreign Affairs*, Oct. 1969, p. 10.

2. For an unclassified summary of the Future Security Strategy Study, directed by Dr. Fred S. Hoffman, see Reading 2.

3. According to Gen. James Abrahamson, "When they [the Russians] see that we have embarked on a long-term effort to achieve an extremely effective defense, supported by a strong national will, they will give up on deployment of more offensive missiles. . . ." *Science*, Aug. 10, 1984, p. 598.

CHAPTER 6

The President's Choice: Star Wars or Arms Control

McGeorge Bundy, George F. Kennan, Robert S. McNamara, and Gerard Smith

* * *

This new initiative was launched by the President on March 23, 1983, in a surprising and quite personal passage at the end of a speech in praise of his other military programs. In that passage he called on our scientists to find means of rendering nuclear weapons "impotent and obsolete." . . .

What is centrally and fundamentally wrong with the President's objective is that it cannot be achieved. The overwhelming consensus of the nation's technical community is that in fact there is no prospect whatever that science and technology can, at any time in the next several decades, make nuclear weapons "impotent and obsolete." The program developed over the last 18 months, ambitious as it is, offers no prospect for a leak-proof defense against strategic ballistic missiles alone, and it entirely excludes from its range any effort to limit the effectiveness of other systems—bomber aircraft, cruise missiles, and smuggled warheads. . . .

The second line of defense for the Star Wars program, and the one which represents the real hopes and convictions of both military men and civilians at the levels below the optimistic President and his enthusiastic secretary of defense, is not that it will ever be able to defend *all our people*, but rather that it will allow us to defend *some of our weapons and other military assets*, and so, somehow, restrain the arms race.

This objective is very different from the one the President has held out to the country, but it is equally unattainable. The Star Wars program is bound to exacerbate the competition between the superpowers in three major ways. It will destroy the Anti-Ballistic Missile (ABM) Treaty, our most important arms control agreement; it will directly stimulate both offensive and defensive systems on the Soviet side; and as long as it continues it

Excerpted by permission of *Foreign Affairs*, Volume 63, No. 2 (Winter 1984/85). Copyright (1985) by the Council on Foreign Relations, Inc.

will darken the prospect for significant improvement in the currently frigid relations between Moscow and Washington. It will thus sharpen the very anxieties the President wants to reduce.

As presented to Congress last March, the Star Wars program calls for a five-year effort of research and development at a total cost of $26 billion. The Administration insists that no decision has been made to develop or deploy any component of the potential system, but a number of hardware demonstrations are planned, and it is hoped that there can be an affirmative decision on full-scale system development in the early 1990s. By its very nature, then, the program is both enormous and very slow. This first $26 billion, only for research and development, is not much less than the full procurement cost of the new B-1 bomber force, and the timetable is such that Mr. Reagan's second term will end long before any deployment decision is made. Both the size and the slowness of the undertaking reinforce the certainty that it will stimulate the strongest possible Soviet response. Its size makes it look highly threatening, while its slowness gives plenty of time for countermeasures.

Meanwhile, extensive American production of offensive nuclear weapons will continue. The Administration has been at pains to insist that the Star Wars program in no way reduces the need for six new offensive systems. There are now two new land-based missiles, two new strategic bombers, and two different submarine systems under various stages of development. The Soviets regularly list several other planned American deployments as strategic because the weapons can reach the Soviet homeland. Mr. Reagan recognized at the very outset that "if paired with offensive systems," any defensive systems "can be viewed as fostering an aggressive policy, and no one wants that." But that is exactly how his new program, with its proclaimed emphasis on both offense and defense, is understood in Moscow.

We have been left in no doubt as to the Soviet opinion of Star Wars. Only four days after the President's speech, Yuri Andropov gave the Soviet reply:

On the face of it, laymen may find it even attractive as the President speaks about what seem to be defensive measures. But this may seem to be so only on the face of it and only to those who are not conversant with these matters. In fact the strategic offensive forces of the United States will continue to be developed and upgraded at full tilt and along quite a definite line at that, namely that of acquiring a first nuclear strike capability. Under these conditions the intention to secure itself the possibility of destroying with the help of the ABM defenses the corresponding strategic systems of the other side, that is of rendering it unable of dealing a retaliatory strike, is a bid to disarm the Soviet Union in the face of the U.S. nuclear threat.[1]

The only remarkable elements in this response are its clarity and rapidity. Andropov's assessment is precisely what we should expect. Our government, of course, does not intend a first strike, but we are building systems which do have what is called in our own jargon a prompt hard-target kill capability, and the primary purpose of these systems is to put Soviet missiles at risk of quick destruction. Soviet leaders are bound to see such weapons as a first-strike threat. This is precisely the view that our own planners take of Soviet missiles with a similar capability. When the President launches a defensive program openly aimed at making Soviet missiles "impotent," while at the same time our own hard-target killers multiply, we cannot be surprised that a man like Andropov saw a threat "to disarm the Soviet Union."[2] Given Andropov's assessment, the Soviet response to Star Wars is certain to be an intensification of both its offensive and defensive strategic efforts.

Perhaps the easiest way to understand this political reality is to consider our own reaction to any similar Soviet announcement of intent. The very thought that the Soviet Union might plan to deploy effective strategic defenses would certainly produce a most energetic American response, and the first and most important element of that response would be a determination to ensure that a sufficient number of our own missiles would always get through.

Administration spokesmen continue to talk as if somehow the prospect of American defensive systems will in and of itself lead the Soviet government to move away from strategic missiles. This is a vain hope. Such a result might indeed be conceivable if Mr. Reagan's original dream were real—if we could somehow ever deploy a *perfect* defense. But in the real world no system will ever be leak-proof; no new system of any sort is in prospect for a decade and only a fragmentary capability for years thereafter; numerous powerful countermeasures are readily available in the meantime, and what is at stake from the Russian standpoint is the deterrent value of their largest and strongest offensive forces.

In this real world it is preposterous to suppose that Star Wars can produce anything but the most determined Soviet effort to make it fruitless. Dr. James Fletcher, chairman of an Administration panel that reviewed the technical prospects after the President's speech, has testified that "the ultimate utility . . . of this system will depend not only on the technology itself, but on the extent to which the Soviet Union agrees to mutual defense arrangements and offense limitations." The plain implication is that the Soviet Union can reduce the "utility" of Star Wars by refusing just such concessions. That is what we would do, and that is what they will do.

Some apologists for Star Wars, although not the President, now defend it on the still more limited ground that it can deny the Soviets a first-strike capability. That is conceivable, in that the indefinite proliferation of systems and countersystems would certainly create fearful uncertainties of all sorts on both sides. But as the Scowcroft Commission correctly concluded, the Soviets have no first-strike capability today, given our survivable forces and the ample existing uncertainties in any surprise attack. We believe there are much better ways than strategic defense to ensure that this situation is maintained. Even a tightly limited and partially effective local defense of missile fields—itself something vastly different from Star Wars—would require radical amendment or repudiation of the ABM Treaty and would create such interacting fears of expanding defenses that we strongly believe it should be avoided.

The President seems aware of the difficulty of making the Soviet Union accept his vision, and he has repeatedly proposed a solution that combines surface plausibility and intrinsic absurdity in a way that tells a lot about what is wrong with Star Wars itself. Mr. Reagan says we should give the Russians the secret of defense, once we find it, in return for their agreement to get rid of nuclear weapons. But the only kind of secret that could be used this way is one that exists only in Mr. Reagan's mind: a single magic formula that would make each side durably invulnerable. In the real world any defensive system will be an imperfect complex of technological and operational capabilities, full understanding of which would at once enable any adversary to improve his own methods of penetration. To share this kind of secret is to destroy its own effectiveness. . . .

There is simply no escape from the reality that Star Wars offers not the promise of greater safety, but the certainty of a large-scale expansion of both offensive and defensive systems on both sides. We are not here examining the dismayed reaction of our allies in Europe, but it is precisely this prospect that they foresee, in addition to the special worries created by their recognition that the Star Wars program as it stands has nothing in it for them. Star Wars, in sum, is a prescription not for ending or limiting the threat of nuclear weapons, but for a competition unlimited in expense, duration and danger. . . . The President's program, because of the inevitable Soviet reaction to it, has already had a heavily damaging impact on prospects for any early progress in strategic arms control. It has thrown a wild card into a game already impacted by mutual suspicion and by a search on both sides for unattainable unilateral advantage. It will soon threaten the very existence of the ABM Treaty.

That treaty outlaws any Star Wars defense. Research is permitted, but the development of space-based systems cannot go beyond the laboratory stage without breaking the Treaty. That would be a most fateful step. We strongly agree with the finding of the Scowcroft Commission, in its final report of March 1984, that "the strategic implications of ballistic missile defense and the criticality of the ABM Treaty to further arms control agreements dictate extreme caution in proceeding to engineering development in this sensitive area."

The ABM Treaty stands at the very center of the effort to limit the strategic arms race by international agreements. It became possible when the two sides recognized that the pursuit of defensive systems would inevitably lead to an expanded competition and to greater insecurity for both. In its underlying meaning, the Treaty is a safeguard less against defense as such than against unbridled competition. The continuing and excessive competition that still exists in offensive weapons would have been even worse without the ABM Treaty, which removed from the calculations of both sides any fear of an early and destabilizing defensive deployment. The consequence over the following decade was profoundly constructive. Neither side attempted a defensive deployment that predictably would have given much more fear to the adversary than comfort to the possessor. The ABM Treaty, in short, reflected a common understanding of exactly the kinds of danger with which Star Wars now confronts the world. To lose the Treaty in pursuit of the Star Wars mirage would be an act of folly.

The defense of the ABM Treaty is thus a first requirement for all who wish to limit the damage done by the Star Wars program. Fortunately the Treaty has wide public support, and the Administration has stated that it plans to do nothing in its five-year program that violates any Treaty clause. Yet by its very existence the Star Wars effort is a threat to the future of the ABM Treaty, and some parts of the announced five-year program raise questions of Treaty compliance. The current program envisions a series of hardware demonstrations, and one of them is described as "an advanced boost-phase detection and tracking system." But the ABM Treaty specifically forbids both the development and the testing of any "space-based" components of an anti-ballistic missile system. We find it hard to see how a boost-phase detection system could be anything but space-based, and we are not impressed by the Administration's claim that such a system is not sufficiently significant to be called "a component." . . .

. . . Congress can readily get the help of advisers drawn from among the many outstanding experts whose judgment has not been silenced or muted by co-option. Such use of independent counselors is one means of repairing the damage done by the President's unfortunate decision to launch his initiative without the benefit of any serious and unprejudiced scientific assessment.

The Congress should also encourage the Administration toward a new and more vigorous effort to insist on respect for the ABM Treaty by the Soviet government as well. Sweeping charges of Soviet cheating on arms control agreements are clearly overdone. It is deeply unimpressive, for example, to catalogue asserted violations of agreements which we ourselves have refused to ratify. But there is one quite clear instance of large-scale construction that does not appear to be consistent with the ABM Treaty— a large radar in central Siberia near the city of Krasnoyarsk. This radar is not yet in operation, but the weight of technical judgment is that it is designed for the detection of incoming missiles, and the ABM Treaty, in order to forestall effective missile defense systems, forbade the erection of such early warning radars except along the borders of each nation. A single highly vulnerable radar installation is of only marginal importance in relation to any large-scale breakout from the ABM Treaty, but it does raise exactly the kinds of questions of intentional violation which are highly destructive in this country to public confidence in arms control.

On the basis of informed technical advice, we think the most likely purpose of the Krasnoyarsk radar is to give early warning of any attack by submarine-based U.S. missiles on Soviet missile fields. Soviet military men, like some of their counterparts in our own country, appear to believe that the right answer to the threat of surprise attack on missiles is a policy of launch-under-attack, and in that context the Krasnoyarsk radar, which fills an important gap in Soviet warning systems, becomes understandable. Such understanding does not make the radar anything else but a violation of the express language of the Treaty, but it does make it a matter which can be discussed and resolved without any paralyzing fear that it is a clear first signal of massive violations yet to come. Such direct and serious discussion with the Soviets might even allow the two sides to consider together the intrinsic perils in a common policy of launch-under-attack. But no such sensitive discussions will be possible while Star Wars remains a non-negotiable centerpiece of American strategic policy. . . .

This has not been a cheerful analysis, or one that we find pleasant to present. If the President makes no major change of course in his second term, we see no alternative to a long, hard, damage-limiting effort by Congress. But we choose to end on a quite different note. We believe that any American president who has won reelection in this nuclear age is bound to ask himself with the greatest seriousness just what he wants to accomplish in his second term. We have no doubt of the deep sincerity of President Reagan's desire for good arms control agreements with the Soviet Union, and we believe his election night assertion that what he wants most in foreign affairs is to reach just such agreements. We are also convinced that if he asks serious and independent advisers what changes in current American policy will help most to make such agreements possible in the next four years, he will learn that it is possible to reach good agreements, or possible to insist on the Star Wars program as it stands, but wholly impossible to do both. At exactly that point, we believe, Mr. Reagan could, should, and possibly would encourage the serious analysis of his negotiating options that did not occur in his first term.

We do not here explore these possibilities in detail. They would certainly include a reaffirmation of the ABM Treaty, and an effort to improve it by broadening its coverage and tightening some of its language. There should also be a further exploration of the possibility of an agreement that would safeguard the peaceful uses of space, uses that have much greater value to us than to the Soviets. We still need and lack a reliable cap on strategic warheads, and while Mr. Reagan has asked too much for too little in the past, he is right to want reductions. He currently has some advisers who fear all forms of arms control, but advisers can be changed. We are not suggesting that the President will change his course lightly. We simply believe that he does truly want real progress on arms control in his second term, and that if he ever comes to understand that he must choose between the two, he will choose the pursuit of agreement over the demands of Star Wars.

We have one final deep and strong belief. We think that if there is to be a real step away from nuclear danger in the next four years, it will have to begin at the level of high politics, with a kind of communication between Moscow and Washington that we have not seen for more than a decade. One of the most unfortunate aspects of the Star Wars initiative is that it was launched without any attempt to discuss it seriously, in advance, with the Soviet government. It represented an explicit expression of the President's belief that we should abandon the shared view of nuclear defense that underlies not only the ABM Treaty but all our later negotiations on strategic weapons. To make a public announcement of a change of this magnitude without any effort to discuss it with the Soviets was to ensure increased Soviet suspicion. This error, too, we have made in earlier decades. If we are now to have renewed hope of arms control, we must sharply elevate our attention to the whole process of communication with Moscow. . . . Alone among the presidents of the last 12 years, Ronald Reagan has the political strength to lead our country in this new direction if he so decides. The renewal of hope cannot be left to await another president without an appeal to the President and his more sober advisers to take a fresh hard look at Star Wars, and then to seek arms control instead.

NOTES

1. Cited in Sidney D. Drell, Philip J. Farley, and David Holloway, *The Reagan Strategic Defense Initiative: A Technical, Political, and Arms Control Assessment*, A Special Report of the Center for International Security and Arms Control, July 1984, Stanford: Stanford University, 1984, p. 105.

2. Richard Nixon has analyzed the possible impact of new defensive systems in even more striking terms: "Such systems would be destabilizing if they provided a shield so that you could use the sword." *Los Angeles Times*, July 1, 1984.

CHAPTER 7

The Case for Strategic Defense: An Option for a World Disarmed

George A. Keyworth II

. . . I feel uncomfortable . . . with reasoning that says that mutual offensive deterrence—*wherein the promise of complete national destruction is presumed*—must remain as policy ad infinitum. I believe we must consider a transition.

I say this for several reasons. First, there is great concern among military analysts about the imbalance between the projected scale of loss in the United States versus that of the Soviet Union as a result of nuclear war. Make no mistake, the results on either side would be catastrophic. But differences in socioeconomic assets; the locations, density, structure, discipline, and civil defense of the populations; and weapon types, numbers, and targeting strategies all combine to produce reasonable estimates that the Soviets might expect 30 to 35 million casualties, while the United States could experience numbers four to five times that. . . .

Because we have relied so heavily on offensive nuclear weapons, an aura of inevitability surrounds them, especially the ballistic missile. The Soviets have used this to great advantage to build a strategic force in which the intercontinental ballistic missile (ICBM) represents 75 percent of their capability. With its speed, increasing accuracy, and incredible payload, the Soviet ICBM fleet has six times the payload capacity of that of the United States.

Soviet reluctance to even discuss real limitations on this ICBM fleet points out the gulf between U.S. and Soviet views. We consider the use of nuclear weapons as unthinkable other than as a retaliatory *deterrent*—that is, to prevent war. The Soviet Union tends to regard nuclear weapons, and the ICBM in particular, more as a *preemptive* means by which to drastically curtail any retaliatory reprisal in the event of war.

Excerpted by permission of *Issues in Science and Technology*, Vol. I, Fall 1984.

The problem is compounded by the imbalance in allied and Soviet conventional forces. The Soviets have more than twice the combat divisions and related equipment and more than three times the tanks and artillery than does the United States. We must therefore contend not only with the possibility of strategic war with mismatched forces, but also with the difficulties of a conventional war occurring under the nuclear umbrella. Given a Soviet doctrine emphasizing both surprise and preemption, the distinction between conventional and nuclear war could blur very rapidly.

Perhaps more than any other person today, President Reagan appreciates this danger. But withdrawal from confrontation—and from our commitment to NATO—is out of the question, as is the unilateral discard of tactical or strategic deterrence. Nor can he or NATO consider massive conventional growth to match the Soviets. The fact remains, however, that today the Soviets are, for all intents and purposes, on a war footing. And while the West regards its nuclear force as retaliatory, the Warsaw Pact nations regard *both* U.S. and Soviet forces as preemptive. This situation can only be viewed as explosive.

Token arms control does absolutely nothing to reduce either the dangers or projected effects of nuclear war. Freezing the present posture only exacerbates the problem. And unilateral or unverifiable agreements are tantamount to suicide. We must take concerted action to maintain our balance on the nuclear wolf while we search for ways to get off it entirely. To do this we must drastically reduce both the utility of nuclear weapons and our reliance upon them. If we succeed, we will have our first real opportunity to bring about deep reductions in the two arsenals. President Reagan directed that we investigate just these options in his March 23 speech of a year ago. . . .

The public sees itself trapped by weapons of mass destruction, a de facto policy of guaranteed delivery, and a de facto policy of massive retaliation. They perceive that both sides maintain a preemptive capability to curtail the damage of a retaliatory strike, that we proliferate our offensive weapons as a counter to preemption, and that proliferation and preemptive capabilities lead to increasing instability. . . .

Do we want to abandon deterrence? Even though many critics may state that those of us who advocate strategic defense are calling for such a policy, there is no question that we must retain a specific retaliatory capability. Nuclear weapons, because of their small size-to-destruction ratio, are a most precious commodity. The destruction resulting from just one weapon is so high that countries might consider any means to acquire one. Ultimately, the issue for countries considering initiating nuclear war is: Is it worth it?

Are the gains worth the risk of retaliation? I propose that if there were no risk of retaliation, then the chances that nuclear weapons might be used would be even greater than they are today. Even if one were to have perfect defenses, an overt no-retaliation posture would be precisely the fatal-fascination-of-the-fortress that has proved disastrous throughout history.

But do we have to maintain nuclear weapons as part of this posture? To retain its credibility, retaliation must balance itself against the potential damage that an enemy can inflict. Unless and until the world can completely rid itself of nuclear weapons, an admittedly unlikely prospect, the nuclear weapon will remain one aspect of any deterrent policy. But I submit that the *massive* retaliatory arsenals that threaten our future today can be made effectively obsolete if the defense technologies we can now foresee are allowed to emerge and evolve.

I propose here a central thesis: It is not deterrence, per se, that has caused the general public to lose faith in our policy and that has caused the buildup of our offensive weapons to turn cancerous. Rather, it is our deliberate and continued inability to protect the socioeconomic structure of our society—coupled with our growing inability to protect the retaliatory deterrent.

. . . The most immediate argument in favor of developing active defenses: they remove the preemptive option, both for the Soviet Union and the United States. Growing preemptive capability has been and continues to be the prime factor in the spiraling arms race. In Soviet eyes, U.S. technical know-how in the 1960s and 1970s provided a unique qualitative edge for preemption that could be overcome only by sheer mass and a strategic force that could get at the enemy fast—the ICBM.

In U.S. eyes, this Soviet ICBM force, coupled with its dramatically improving technological performance and survivability, gave the Soviets an overwhelming preemptive potential, unparalleled flexibility, and an unacceptable strategic reserve in times of conflict; hence, the concerted U.S. attempts to modernize its strategic forces starting in the late 1970s. . . .

In reality, the possibility of a disarming first strike is the subject of considerable debate. As Brent Scowcroft pointed out, the U.S. Triad structure mitigates the preemptive aspect of most Soviet attack options—at least for today. The Soviets cannot be sure of completely destroying the U.S. bomber fleet, which carries nearly half our megatonnage, with their ICBMs because the 25- to 30-minute missile flight allows time to get some of our bombers off the ground. While Soviet submarine-launched ballistic missiles (SLBM) might have a good bolt-from-the-blue chance at most of our bombers, they are not now accurate enough to destroy ICBM silos. Moreover, any early SLBM launch to catch the bombers would provide the United States with unmistakable attack confirmation with which to release our ICBMs. In addition, neither Soviet weapons system can now attack U.S. submarines.

Similarly, it is our assessment that U.S. land- and sea-based ballistic missiles are currently unable to completely destroy the Soviet ICBM force; Soviet silos are very hard and our weapons have inadequate accuracy and yield. Our bombers give at least six to eight hours warning time, and like ours, Soviet submarines are presently secure.

But the reader should note two crucial points. First, although the situation may be stable, it is very fragile. Second, the situation will change. Both sides already have the technologies and have initiated the necessary developments for hard-target kill of even the most advanced silos. And while Admiral Gayler advises us to bank on the fact that "our submarines are invulnerable," I would hasten to point out that survivability of our nuclear submarines is a function of how well they can hide. This, in turn, is a function of signal-to-noise in detection devices and also of data processing. Data processing is our most rapidly accelerating technology, the one most sought by the Soviets, and the one most easily researched, developed, tested, and deployed without our knowledge. What's more, the Soviets need not know our exact submarine locations, just their general operating areas. Submarines operating within 100 square miles of a one-megaton underwater explosion would be effectively neutralized. In short, although we retain a viable submarine force now, change is inevitable.

The era of survivability through passive measures, such as hardening of underground facilities, is rapidly drawing to a close. That the offense will always triumph over the defense is debatable, but it is a sure bet that it will if the defense does nothing. One might also consider that, unchecked, these improvements in offensive weapons could foretell the end to arms control because under the measure-countermeasure theory of deterrence, mutually vulnerable offensive forces would have to undergo escalation at an unprecedented rate.

It is time to pursue the technological options for active defense. Significant technological advances have occurred since the last serious debate on ballistic missile defense in the late 1960s. We have before us the prospect of advanced defenses that can provide crisis stability and slam the lid on the MIRV. . . .

We are already in an era when warning and decision times are becoming extremely short. As technology advances during the next decade, those intervals may be reduced to the point at which in times of crisis—or mechanical or human error—a policy of shoot-first-and-ask-questions-later may become an option, a terribly dangerous option, for both sides. At the very least, active defenses can conceivably give us precious time to make those decisions. At best, they can reduce the consequences of an accidental or erroneous launch, nuclear adventures by Third-World countries or madmen, and massive retaliation and the loss of hundreds of thousands of lives. Of possibly greater import, once having made a mistake, the offending country would not automatically have to deal with what I'll call the "failsafe" dilemma—that is, a decision on whether to immediately follow the mistake with a complete nuclear attack rather than face retaliation. Experts, of course, dismiss this possibility. The ordinary citizen has a deep-rooted fear of it.

The prospect of boost-phase defense nullifies MIRV technology as it has now evolved. For the first time, the large Soviet heavy-lift booster, the SS-18, becomes an albatross instead of a workhorse. Fully half the payload of the Soviet fleet becomes obsolete, not overnight, but by-and-by.

Believers in the "ten-foot-tall Russian" quickly counter this argument by trotting out the Soviets' "easily attainable" next generation of the fast-burn, protectively coated, quick-spin booster that cuts the SS-18's 500-second burn time by an order of magnitude. Never mind that the Fletcher study team looked at these same Soviet countermeasures and projected that defense technologies could defeat them. Never mind that their proposed 40- to 50-second burn times still leave the reentry vehicle well inside the atmosphere—thereby requiring a post-boost vehicle that is vulnerable to boost-phase defenses. Never mind that there are a number of directed-energy wavelengths that can reach into the atmosphere just as far as the booster dares burn out. Never mind that if the fast-burn boost is possible at all, it is probably three to five generations away from those ICBMs the Soviets already have in the works. Never mind that it causes the Soviets to completely change directions with a 15-year investment in 75 percent of their strategic force. Never mind that it significantly reduces payload and MIRV capacity.

Strategic defenses of the type we can reasonably project—even in their early modes—can be vital catalysts for arms control. Critics are quick to point out that if any defense system is not perfect, some weapons will unquestionably leak through. In fact, early and intermediate defenses will undoubtedly be imperfect, and any nuclear weapon that makes it through to its target will be devastating. While hardened military assets can be very successfully defended by these transition systems, civilian population centers will still be hostage to a determined adversary. Critics cite this as a major failing. In fact, it is crucial to stability during those transition years because as long as there is some leakage in those transition defense technologies, there remains a retaliatory deterrent against first strike.

We will have effectively turned the clock back 20 years. Some will accuse us of returning to an era when weapons were safe but people were not. Perhaps so. But we will once again have a common ground for negotiating real weapons reductions. After all, realistic, survivable, retaliatory arsenals do not have to be enormous, not nearly as large as the arsenals we now require to survive preemptive srikes (or in the Soviet case, to launch them). With the preemptive option clouded, or even removed, we would have an opportunity to negotiate major arms reductions that would still leave each side with a strong retaliatory deterrent.

At that point we would have accomplished two things, two goals that have eluded us for 20 years. We would have reduced both nations' perceptions that the other could launch a successful disarming first strike, and we would have drastically reduced the size of the arsenals.

Achieving these goals could introduce a new transition period during which conventional military technologies and forces would be rebuilt. This will be the price we pay for moving out from under the nuclear umbrella. At the same time, second- and third-generation defensive technologies would become available. This could further reduce the effectiveness of strategic nuclear weapons to the point that civilian targets could become truly viable candidates for defense.

These options will probably become available when the strategic nuclear forces we must build today to maintain our near-term deterrence reach the limits of their operational lifetimes. We then have a new option: rather than replace them, let each side retain only token nuclear forces for their sole remaining purpose—restricted retaliation.

It is only at this point, in the presence of near-zero arsenals, that arms control begins to have any real meaning in the minds of ordinary people. Only when the prospect of final world holocaust reverts to "mere" catastrophe—that is, when the stockpiles can be measured in the dozens, rather than in the tens of thousands—can we once again depend on the sun coming up the next day.

As Colin Gray has said, this can only happen in the presence of defense: treaties that attempt to draw offensive forces to very low levels are impractical without an insurance policy. Although some policymakers, both liberal or conservative, may publicly espouse truly deep, near-zero reductions in the world's nuclear arsenals, they know these reductions to be impossible, even irresponsible, in a world wherein nations dare not trust one another. A world disarmed would be at the mercy of any state or faction that had concealed only a handful of weapons. In the land of the blind, the one-eyed man is king.

Gray notes that it would be naive to tie comprehensive nuclear disarmament to our adversaries' evolution into trusted democracies. Soviet habits, attitudes, and policies are the product of a thousand years of brutal historical experience. There is no reason to believe that the Soviet Union will suddenly become a country that we would trust to respect the legal requirements of a near-total disarmament treaty. And even were a very un-Soviet U.S.S.R. to emerge, I would still worry about the nonaligned Third World. . . .

Strategic defense provides the option to break this cycle. Although we cannot disinvent nuclear weapons, and although nations will continue to distrust one another, heavily defended countries could nonetheless realistically enter into treaties to reduce nuclear forces to near zero. The scale of cheating necessary to provide an arsenal capable of successfully engaging seveal layers of active defenses would be so large as to be impractical within the context of normal intelligence-gathering capabilities.

Strategic defense therefore provides an option for a world effectively disarmed of nuclear weapons, yet still retaining national sovereignty and security. In fact, deployment of strategic defense is the only way in which the superpowers will be able to achieve these very deep arms reductions. It now becomes extremely important to recognize that the ballistic missile and air defenses that might look less than 100 percent perfect in the context of an offensive exchange involving tens of thousands of warheads could be expected to perform magnificently against an attack by only tens, or at the most hundreds, of weapons.

I do not offer this scenario lightly. Moving out from under the nuclear umbrella under any circumstance is a serious, sobering, and expensive proposition. Neither our military structure, organization, nor technology is prepared for it now—not strategically or tactically.

Moreover, I must issue one caution. Strategic defense must never be perceived as a technological panacea. It is a tool, a catalyst, nothing more. The roots of our security problems are political. However, pending a benign transformation in the ways of the world, it behooves us to invest in a military capability that increases the prospects for meaningful arms control and gives hope to those that follow us.

Admittedly, there are many "if's" in the prospects for strategic defense. But the president proposed that we use our ingenuity to pursue these defensive technologies, and outstanding scientists substantiate his faith. It is our obligation—our responsibility—to provide new options for our political leaders.

We cannot look down each other's gun barrels indefinitely, regardless of the rational balance we think we can maintain. Rational men have rarely started history's wars. Nor can we play into the Soviets' strong suit—men and materiel. Instead, we must start to play our trump—technological leverage. We must move rapidly to develop the means to both reduce our own reliance on tactical and strategic nuclear weapons and the Soviets' perception that either side could use them to advantage. And we must couple these technical moves with negotiations for deep reductions in nuclear weapons. We must begin our transition from the 1950s to the year 2000. And we must offer hope that we can achieve a world free of the fear of nuclear war.

CHAPTER 8

A Case for Strategic Defense

Colin S. Gray

There is need for a forward-looking debate on strategic defence. Unfortunately, the attitude of many people towards this subject was forged fifteen or more years ago, and their minds are not open to new possibilities. For example, there is a widespread tendency to consider the ABM (anti-ballistic missile) Treaty sacrosanct, forgetting what arms control is all about. Arms control, first and above all else, is about reducing the risks of war—that overriding goal may or may not be served by a particular, formal treaty regime. If an arms-control treaty precludes weapons development and deployment that should reduce first-strike incentives, then that treaty does not function as an arms-control measure.

The ABM Treaty of 1972, as amended in 1974, reflected contemporary predictions concerning probable trends in strategic offensive forces that have not been borne out by events. . . .

THE SDI: WHAT IT IS, AND WHAT IT IS NOT

What is the SDI? It should be (a) an exploration of ways in which the stability of the *existing* system of offensive, retaliatory deterrence might be enhanced: (b) an exploration of ways in which the terms of deterrence might be transformed in favour of much greater safety for civilians everywhere; and it should be recognized as (c) the only remotely feasible path by which nuclear disarmament on a truly massive scale might be secured.

The SDI is *not* (a) yet a weapons programme; (b) a promise that society as a whole can for certain be defended directly; (c) a quest after some ever-elusive, illusory 'ultimate weapon' (such cannot exist); nor is it (d) a promise of political peace.

Excerpted from *Survival*, March-April 1985 (London: International Institute for Strategic Studies, 1985). The article is a revised version of a prepared statement delivered before the Subcommittee on Strategic and Theater Nuclear Forces of the Senate Armed Services Committee on April 24, 1984.

Lest the point be lost in subsequent discussion, it might be emphasized that Soviet-American rivalry is political in its origins, is fuelled overwhelmingly by political anxieties and ambitions, and can be alleviated or resolved only by political action. Those who, like this author, strongly favour the possibilities inherent in the SDI are under no illusions about the limitations of a 'technological peace.' Even if the SDI should prove to be a magnificent technological success story, which—looking forward 20 or 30 years from now—is certainly possible, strategic defence will not be a panacea for deeply political security problems. The SDI and a defensive transition can change the terms of deterrence, away from retaliatory nuclear threat (which would be no small accomplishment), but, in and of itself, it cannot arrest the arms competition. The 'last move' in that competition must be political, not military-technological. . . . A very major portion of the case for proceeding with the SDI is the virtually self-evident fact that there are no attractive alternative paths to greater security.

Eventually, the Soviet-American rivalry will be resolved, hopefully by formal or tacit political agreement rather than by military decision. However, historically speaking, all security systems break down or are transformed as conditions change. The nuclear deterrence system familiar today, with very dominant offensive capabilities, is adequate all the time that it either functions as we intend or, as generally is the case, all the time that it is not severely tested. The problem, indeed the enduring problem, is that the future rests upon a nuclear deterrence system concerning which even a single serious malfunction cannot be tolerated. So 40 years into the nuclear age it is uncertain whether the absence of bilateral nuclear war should be attributed more to luck than to sound policy. The question is, for how long should this system of reciprocated nuclear retaliatory threats be expected to work satisfactorily? One may be confident that stability reigns today, but how confident can one be for the next 50 or 100 years?

The SDI and a defensive transition cannot effect a benign transformation in the politics of East-West competition, but it *may*, and only *may*, serve to buy time for the alleviation and resolution of political differences. At the very least, it would be grossly irresponsible and imprudent to refuse the challenge to try to live in greater safety with nuclear weapons that cannot be disinvented.

Before discussing transition issues in some detail, it is important that the range of choice available be appreciated. If one rejects the very idea of strategic defence one is, *ipso facto,* endorsing the seemingly endless competition in offensive nuclear arms. The alternative to the SDI is not a happy world of super-stable, jointly well-managed offensive arsenals; instead it is a world of acute competition and anxiety over net war-fighting prowess that cannot withstand a single breakdown in the extant deterrence system. Not only is strategic defence not an alternative to disarmament, strategic defence is the only way by which nuclear disarmament worthy of the name might be achieved. In the absence of defence, no one knows how to achieve nuclear disarmament on a scale such that civilization, and even the ecosphere itself, would not be at prompt or delayed fatal risk in the event of a failure of deterrence. Even the US 'build-down' proposal[1] in START—which the Soviet Union has rejected in very unflattering terms (describing it in *Pravda* as being 'designed for fools'[2])—would leave the super-powers with truly massive nuclear arsenals.

If one is serious about nuclear disarmament, as one should be, and given that no one knows how to achieve a general political settlement with the Soviet Union that would render issues of competitive nuclear armament politically irrelevant, there is no prudent choice available other than to press on carefully to explore the possibilities of strategic defence. Only in the presence of multi-layered strategic defences would the super-powers be able to endorse a very radical scale of nuclear disarmament. With such defences, East and West could live with a disarmament treaty that would not be verifiable with absolute confidence. In the absence of homeland defences, the incentive to cheat on a disarmament regime would be matched only by the ease with which the Soviet Union could cheat.

Far distant though nuclear disarmament may be, it is morally and politically essential that the US government should be able to articulate a not-implausible theory of how such disarmament might be effected in ways compatible with US and US-allied security. This theory should be an integral part of the policy story for the SDI, notwithstanding the proximate necessity for having a very prudent and robust appreciation of the difficulties attendant upon proceeding from here to there.

MANAGING A DEFENSIVE TRANSITION

It is always possible that as a consequence of focusing upon the shape of distant woods one may walk into a tree or two in the foreground. One can hardly stress too much the importance of approaching and managing a process of defensive transition with extreme care, while it is essential that the US (and her allies) understands whither it would like to proceed in the long term with strategic defence, there is everything to be said in favour of being cautious lest the price of the journey to a directly defended Western Alliance be an increased risk of war along the way.

Whatever may or may not be possible eventually by way of the active defence of cities, the first necessary steps must be the intermediate capabilities emphasized in the Hoffman Report[3] for the protection of US retaliatory forces and C^3I assets. These capabilities would comprise necessary under-layers for what might one day become a comprehensive architecture of (multi-) nation-wide defence. But whether or not it proves feasible to destroy ballistic missiles in their 'boost-phase' or 'post-boost-phase' terminal non-nuclear defences could provide a very attractive and effective way of strengthening strategic stability. Such defences would have to promote massive new uncertainties in Soviet attack calculations—calculations that already are beset with major technical, tactical, strategic and political uncertainties. American (and NATO-European) policy-makers in the 1990s should be provided with active defence alternatives, or partial alternatives, to the proliferation of offensive weapons, the proliferation of aim points through mobility, and the adoption of dangerous launch tactics. There is no need to decide today whether the US will exercise such intermediate defensive options, but the case for purchasing the ability to choose in a timely fashion would seem to be overwhelming.

Probably the single most frequent objection that is raised to the nearer-term aspects of the SDI and a defensive transition is that it will 'stimulate the arms race'. This objection is really no more than a truism. Any US strategic-force development which threatens to thwart some aspects of Soviet strategy, to deny some measure of military advantage, may serve as fuel for Soviet competitive behaviour. There are some interesting co-operative possibilities for a defensive transition, but those possibilities can rest only upon effective US competitive performance. The Soviet Union certainly will be motivated to seek to dissuade the US from pursuing the SDI and an effective defensive transition. Dissuasion will take the forms of weapon development optimized for penetration of defences and, very likely, of arms-control blandishments.

THE SDI AND ARMS CONTROL

Should the US decide to move with the SDI from technology exploration into weapon development, formal arms-control negotiations could assume great importance. First, late in the 1980s the US may wish to renegotiate the terms of the ABM Treaty so as to permit development and limited deployment of defences for strategic forces and strategic C³I facilities. American policy-makers would confront a choice that relates to the heart of deterrence reasoning. Should they seek an arms-control regime that would assist the pre-launch survivability of nuclear forces, though at the price of impeded access—courtesy of Soviet deployments of ballistic missile defences—to Soviet territory? Or, should the ABM Treaty be retained in its pristine form, at the price of denying US forces and C³I a potentially valuable measure of prelaunch survivability? In the opinion of this author it would be wise to choose pre-launch survivability rather than unimpeded access.

Second, later in the 1990s, or perhaps early in the next century, the opportunity could arise for a truly radical, benign restructuring of strategic forces through the arms-control process. While the effectiveness of a US defensive transition can never be permitted to hinge upon co-operation with the Soviet Union—for the obvious reason that they seek military advantage, and certainly they seek to deny any military advantage to the US—there is no doubt that a large-scale reduction in the quantity of Soviet offensive forces, not to mention some qualitative restraints upon the forces that remained, would enhance greatly the prospective performance of strategic defenses. So, the problem then, as today, is one of negotiating leverage. President Reagan's vision of a much reduced scale of nuclear threat is more likely to be achievable if the Soviet Union can be brought to believe that nuclear disarmament on a massive scale is in her net security interest. This will not be a matter of strategic theoretical persuasion, of lectures on the new US theory of stability through dominant defences, or of devising ingenious formulae for reciprocal reductions. Stated directly, Soviet leaders and strategic planners will need to look at the actual and the potential of US competitive performance in defensive and offensive weaponry, and decide that they face an important military disadvantage if they choose to let the competition run its course in a legally unregulated fashion.

By way of a contingent prediction, if Soviet leaders believe that US offensive forces will fare considerably better against Soviet defences than will Soviet offensive forces against US defences, then they should be motivated to agree to negotiated reductions in offensive forces. In American perspective, given that the US is far more interested in protecting Americans that she is in threatening Soviet citizens, the US should be prepared to forgo some measure of military advantage conferred by the superior penetrative prowess of her offensive forces, as a price well worth paying for the reduction in the scale and quality of the Soviet offensive threat.

NUCLEAR AMBUSH OF A DEFENSIVE TRANSITION?

Some critics of the SDI have expressed concern that, should the Soviet Union anticipate the US achieving a significant military advantage through defensive deployments, she may elect to take very forceful measures to prevent a US defensive transition, or addition, from maturing. Several responses to this valid concern are appropriate, but the leading one is to the effect that it must be a mission of the strategic offensive forces to guard the defensive transition. . . .

The nightmare scenario of a desperate Soviet Union choosing to fight today rather than live with the consequences of a measure of military inferiority tomorrow, is thoroughly implausible, if not totally ridiculous. Should Soviet leaders anticipate military disadvantage as the defensive transitions (on both sides) mature, the extant US offensive force posture, if properly modernised, would provide them with the most persuasive of reasons for eschewing prompt military adventure. Even if the military balance tomorrow looks likely to be worse than that today, the balance today is most unlikely to offer a good prospect of success. Furthermore, Soviet leaders will have an attractive alternative both to suicide today and to inferiority tomorrow—and that is a defensive competition managed by arms control.

The point should not be missed that the earliest US deployment action during a transition to defences will be systems for the defence of strategic retaliatory forces and C³I. That deployment must function so as to discourage any Soviet theorizing about a nuclear ambush of a US defensive transition. . . .

THE SDI AND THE WESTERN ALLIANCE

Critics of the SDI are able to point, accurately enough, to some disquiet in NATO-Europe over what US strategic defence developments may imply for East-West relations and for US motives and prospective performance as a security guarantor. Space precludes detailed treatment of this issue here, but the following points are relevant:

• Near-term strategic defence developments, for the enhancement of the pre-launch survivability of US strategic forces, would simply strengthen the familiar terms of nuclear deterrence.
• Near-term, point-defence technology, if deployed in Europe, would greatly strengthen the stability of deterrence. Anti-tactical ballistic missile (ATBM) defence against shorter-range Soviet missiles would deny the Soviet Union an important measure of confidence concerning the prospects for conventional success. ATBM defence of NATO airfields, supply dumps, C^3 facilities, transportation nodes and the like would play a literally vital role in facilitating the defence of NATO-Europe and, *ergo*, in discouraging aggression.
• Far-term defensive technology (probably space-based, or space-deployable) could protect US allies as well as the US herself. Moreover, it we can move into an era wherein the American homeland enjoys a growing measure of direct, physical protection, the willingness of US presidents to run risks on behalf of distant allies logically should be strengthened. Far from being an instrument with 'decoupling' implications, strategic defence would work to enhance solidarity of behaviour in crisis and war.
• Soviet strategic missile defences must work to challenge the credibility of the small national deterrents of France and Britain. . . . To the end of the century, and probably beyond, the French and British national deterrents would retain sufficient potential to 'leak through' Soviet defences that they would not face an immediate crisis of technical relevance. For the longer term, should both super-powers proceed to deploy heavy, multi-tiered nation-wide defences, then small nuclear forces, no matter how sophisticated their penetration aids, would indeed lack credibility. Given the benefits of a defensive transition in strategic forces, and the likely very high scale of effectiveness of theatre and tactical missile defences, NATO-European countries should welcome the opportunity to be able to devote their attention wholeheartedly to the problems of local conventional deterrence.

CONCLUSIONS

No one can say what the balance of technological and tactical advantage between offence and defence will be in 20 or 30 years. But we do know that the history of military technology records swings of the pendulum of advantage from one to the other; and that strategic offensive technologies today are relatively mature, while strategic defensive technologies are very immature—meaning that for the next several decades at least the advantage in growth in performance potential ought plain to lie with the defence.

Lest there be any misunderstanding, this author is *not* predicting particular weapons, for particular missions, by particular dates, with particular costs. There is no way of knowing whether multi-tiered strategic defences capable of rendering ICBM and SLBM as obsolete as the horse cavalry will be technologically feasible. But, there is a major, indeed an overwhelming, arms-control case for investment in the SDI to explore the possibility that the defence could reassume a position of strategic pre-eminence. . . .

It must be acknowledged that the West faces a sharply growing threat from Soviet air-breathing vehicles. Hence, a defensive transition, to have strategic integrity, must include air as well as missile defences. Also, it would be foolish to ignore the unfortunate fact that the strategic nuclear deterrent does have a range of specific missions of the highest importance for foreign policy. If the political structure of Soviet-American relations remains much as today, then there will be a need to find strategic substitutes for the nuclear threat to the Soviet homeland. Even in the context of a mature defensive transition, the Soviet Union will still need to be deterred from pursuing military solutions to her most pressing political problems.

NOTES

1. 'Build-down' would require the dismantling of more than one older strategic warhead for each new warhead deployed. For descriptions of the various 'build-down' concepts, see Alton Frye, "Strategic Build-down: A Context for Restraint', *Foreign Affairs*, Winter 1983/84, vol. 62, no. 2, pp. 293–317; and 'Negotiating a Build-down', *Time*, 17 October 1983, pp. 16–18.

2. 'Bogus Flexibility But Real Deception', *Pravda*, 23 October 1983, as translated by the Federal Broadcast Information Service, *Daily Report: USSR*, 24 October 1983, p. AA6.

3. Fred S. Hoffman (Study Director), *Ballistic Missile Defenses and US National Security*, Summary Report of the Future Security Strategy Study (Washington DC: October 1983).

Bibliography: Part Two

Abrahamson, Lt. General James A. "SDI Program Update." *Defense 86* (January/February, 1986):7–13.

Bethe, Hans A., et al. "Space-Based Ballistic Missile Defense." *Scientific American* (October 1984):39–49.

Blacker, Coit D. "Defending Missiles, Not People: Hard-Site Defense." *Issues in Science and Technology* (Fall 1985):30–44.

Brown, Harold. "The Strategic Defense Initiative: Defensive Systems and the Strategic Debate." *Survival* (March/April 1985):55–64.

Brzezinski, Zbigniew, Robert Jastrow, and Max M. Kampelman. "Defense in Space is Not Star Wars." *New York Times Magazine*, January 27, 1985.

Drell, Sidney D., and Wolfgang K. H. Panofsky. "The Case Against Strategic Defense: Technical and Strategic Realities." *Issues in Science and Technology* (Fall 1984):45–65.

Garwin, Richard L., et al. *The Fallacy of Star Wars.* New York: Random House, 1984.

Garwin, Richard L., et al. "Space Weapons." *Bulletin of the Atomic Scientists,* May 1984.

Jastrow, Robert. "Reagan vs. the Scientists: Why the President is Right about Missile Defense." *Commentary* (January 1984):23–32.

Nitze, Paul H. "The Promise of SDI." U.S. State Department, Bureau of Public Affairs, Current Policy No. 810, March 1986.

Payne, Keith B., and Gray, Colin S. "Nuclear Policy and the Defensive Transition." *Foreign Affairs* (Spring 1984):820–842.

Weinberger, Caspar W. "Strategic Defense in Perspective." *Defense 86* (January/February 1986):2–6.

Yonas, Gerold. "The Reagan Strategic Defense Initiative." *Daedalus* (Spring 1985):73–90.

PART THREE

TECHNICAL FEASIBILITY

Although the partisans for and against hold strong opinions, no one knows at this stage if SDI is technically feasible. In their careful discussion of technical feasibility, Sidney Drell, Philip Farley, and David Holloway show the scope and difficulty of the scientific and engineering problems that must be resolved to make SDI work. They doubt that chemical lasers will be a practical weapon with which to attack enemy missiles during boost-phase because of the huge amounts of fuel needed to supply the hundreds of necessary laser platforms in space. They also doubt that "pop-up" systems—X-ray lasers based on the ground and sent into space at first warning of an attack—can overcome the operational difficulties posed by the short reaction available to catch missiles in boost-phase and the countermeasures an enemy might take, such as converting to fast-burning rocket engines that shut off before the missile has left the atmosphere.

The great attraction of Harold Brown's article is that it avoids the ultimate question and returns the debate to earth by estimating the length of time required to develop and deploy the various kinds of missile defenses under discussion. According to Brown, it would take 15 years to deploy hard-site terminal defense (defending missile silos). During the same period the components of space-based kinetic energy weapons could be developed that would collide or explode against attacking missiles under guidance from satellites. At least a quarter century may be required to develop ground-based lasers for use against attacking missiles. In short, the defense of people rather than missile silos is a matter for the years beyond 2010.

The Fletcher report supplied the scientific backing for a large-scale research effort to explore SDI fully before deciding for or against it. Edward Teller has been an advocate of strategic defense for years and was intimately involved in persuading President Reagan to launch SDI. His enthusiasm and commitment to SDI are evident.

CHAPTER 9

The SDI:
A Technical Appraisal

Sidney D. Drell, Philip J. Farley, and David Holloway

THE LAYERED DEFENSE

Up to the present, the dominance of offense over defense has been based on technical considerations. In recent years the technology pertinent to this problem has advanced significantly. Great strides have been made in the ability to produce, focus, and aim laser and particle beams of increasingly high power. These new "bullets" of directed energy travel at or near the velocity of light and have led to revolutionary new ideas for defense against ballistic missiles. There has also been a revolutionary expansion in our ability to gather, process, and transmit vast quantities of data efficiently and promptly. This makes it possible to provide high quality intelligence from distant parts of the earth and space in order to assess and discriminate the properties of attacks very promptly—i.e., in "real time." The technical advances in the ability to manage a defense and to attack distant targets very quickly have removed a number of shortcomings of previous defense concepts.

Major technical advances have also led to great improvements in the offense. The crucial question that must be addressed is whether technology now offers a new promise of changing the conditions of offense dominance. Although most agree that we cannot now build an effective defense based on what is known today, can we now foresee the possibility of building an effective defensive system; and if so, under what conditions?

The major technical fact that has not changed with time is the overwhelming destructive power of nuclear weapons. To speak, as President Reagan did, of "rendering nuclear weapons impotent and obsolete" by defending one's vital national interests—people, industries, cities—against a

Excerpted by permission of the authors from Sidney D. Drell, Philip J. Farley, and David Holloway, *The Reagan Strategic Defense Initiative: A Technical, Political, and Arms Control Assessment.* A Special Report of the Center for International Security and Arms Control, Stanford University (Stanford, Calif.: International Strategic Institute at Stanford, 1984).

massive nuclear attack still requires a defense that is almost perfect. Technical assessments of ABM *concepts* cannot escape this awesome *systems* requirement. If but 1 percent of the approximately 8,000 nuclear warheads on the current Soviet force of land-based and sea-based ballistic missiles succeeded in penetrating a defensive shield and landed on urban targets in the U.S., it would be one of the greatest disasters in all history!

Many components form a defensive system against ballistic missiles, and all are crucial to its effective operation. These include the sensors providing early warning of an attack; the communication links for conveying that information to analysis centers for interpretation, to the command centers with authority to make decisions as to the appropriate national response, and to the military forces to implement the decisions; the sensors of the ABM that acquire, discriminate, track, point, fire, and assess the effectiveness of the attack; and finally the interceptors or directed energy sources that make the kill. The systems for managing the battle and for delivering destructive energy concentrations with precision must be operational at the initiation of an attack and must remain effective throughout. This means being on station, yet being able to survive direct attack. The ability to satisfy these two requirements simultaneously is a major operational challenge. Even if the very ambitious R&D program recently proposed by the Administration achieves all of its major goals, far beyond presently demonstrated technologies, great operational barriers will still remain.

The concept of a "defense-in-depth" has evolved since no single technology alone is adequate to provide an impenetrable defensive shield, or anti-ballistic Maginot Line. . . . The first layer attacks the rising missiles during their boost phase while their engines are burning. Typically, this phase lasts three minutes for modern missiles which are powered by rockets that burn solid fuel, and up to five minutes for liquid fuel boosters. During this time the missile rises above the atmosphere to heights of 200 to 300 kilometers (km). The second (and perhaps third) layer of the defense attacks the warheads, or RVs (reentry vehicles), as well as the post-boost vehicle (which is the small bus that aims and dispenses the individual MIRVs) during their midcourse trajectories lasting about twenty to twenty-five minutes (for ICBMs). The final or terminal layer of the defense attacks the reentry vehicles during the last minute or two of their flight as they reenter the atmosphere which strips away the lighter decoys accompanying them in mid-flight. A three-layer system, each of whose layers is 90 percent effective, would allow only 8 out of an attacking force of 8,000 RVs to arrive on target and would, if achievable, be highly effective, though less than perfect as a defense. . . .

The following subsections will describe the generic technical difficulties that must be surmounted in building such a defensive umbrella. The analysis of the parameters used to characterize specific systems concepts are based on laws of physics and on what is known from open sources. These parameters in no way represent practical or optimal system design numbers. However they are generally very optimistic from the viewpoint of the emerging technology. They are intended to provide "best case" estimates that are useful and valid as a basis for arriving at informed judgments as to the potential practicability of deploying an effective defense against a responsive threat.[1]

BOOST-PHASE INTERCEPT

The possibility of boost-phase intercept is the principal new element in considering ABM technologies. It also has the highest potential payoff for two reasons:

1. Whatever success is achieved in this initial layer of the defense reduces the size of the attacking force to be engaged by each subsequent layer.
2. If a missile is destroyed during boost when it is relatively vulnerable, all of its warheads and decoys are destroyed with it.

Following the missile boost phase, the defense has more time for performing its functions of acquiring and discriminating warheads from decoys, attacking its targets, and confirming their destruction. On the other hand, although not so severely constrained by very short engagement times, it must also cope with many more objects since a single large booster is capable of deploying tens of warheads and many hundreds of decoys. Thus the two defensive layers for boost-phase and for mid-course intercept face very different technological challenges. Moreover, an effective boost-phase layer, which greatly reduces the number of objects that subsequent layers must analyze, attack, and destroy, is crucial to the overall effectiveness of a defensive system.

In order to illustrate the general problems for boost-phase intercept we consider two types of systems, one with interceptors based in space and the other with interceptors based on ground and ready to "pop-up" on receipt of warning of an enemy attack. A hybrid concept with mixed ground and space basing is also discussed. All defensive systems rely on space-based sensors for early warning; for command, control, and communications; and for overall battle management. The combination of tactics and technology to ensure the survival of the space-based components of a defense against direct enemy attack has yet to be developed. It is listed by the Department of Defense as one of the critical problems that "will probably require research and development programs of ten to twenty years to be ready for deployment."[2]

SPACE-BASED CHEMICAL LASERS

One of the most widely discussed systems for boost-phase intercept is a constellation of high energy lasers based on platforms orbiting the earth in space. Very well focused laser beams have the attractive feature for ABM of traveling vast distances with the speed of light in space above the atmosphere. The disadvantages of space-based lasers are that they are complex and expensive, they are vulnerable to attack, there are many effective countermeasures available to the attacker, and generally their beams are degraded by scattering and absorption by the atmosphere and so they must function above it. Furthermore, each platform of any space-based system will be "on station" over the launch area of Soviet ICBMs only a small percentage of the time as it circles the globe in a low earth orbit; i.e., each platform will have a large "absentee ratio." Therefore, it will be inherently inefficient, having to be replicated many times over if the defense is to provide continual protection against ICBM launches. . . .

There are additional generic difficulties for any defensive system for which components are predeployed in space. In addition to specific countermeasures that render them ineffective, their foremost difficulty is that they will most likely be vulnerable to direct enemy attack. Among the simplest direct threats that could be deployed even during the early stages of building up to a full space-based defensive layer are small and relatively cheap space mines with conventional explosives. They could be launched into orbits, and detonated by radio command from ground to damage the large, delicate, and highly vulnerable optical parts. The presence of such space mines would not be covert. They could "shadow" a satellite in a manner similar to that used by ships on the high seas; in particular by Soviet intelligence-gathering ships (which also may be armed) that currently observe our naval battle groups. Of course, the Soviets could also put nuclear bombs in orbit. These would have an enormous range for damage of such systems and their necessarily "almost perfect optics." Ground-based laser beams pose another direct threat to the sensitive optical sensors of such a system. The space-based defenses would have to be prepared to "blink" if so attacked in order to avoid damage, particularly if the incident radiation comes in short, intense pulses.

Not all laser platforms would have to be attacked and put out of action; just a sizable fraction of that small percentage that are on station over the ICBM launch areas during boost phase. The offense can then be confident that a sizable fraction of his attack will penetrate the first layer of the defense. In considering the difficulty of making such space-based systems survivable, it is important to recognize that they are much more delicate (and expensive!) than the individual ICBMs against which they are deployed and, therefore, the task of protecting them is inherently more difficult than that of hardening the ICBMs against them. . . .[3]

Countermeasures other than direct attack include further hardening of the missiles against the incident beam energy. . . . Two approaches are to coat the booster by a somewhat thicker (by a few millimeters) heat shield, or dispense an aerosol to absorb the incident fluence and disperse it harmlessly. Another useful technique is to spin the missile at the rate of a few turns a second during boost so that the beam energy is distributed at lower fluence around the booster surface. There are additional problems that can be created for such a defensive system. Precursor nuclear bursts at high altitudes can precede an attack and disrupt its operations, particularly its sensors and communication links. There is, of course, no spare time available for replacing or reconstituting these components since the entire system must operate within the first few minutes in order to destroy an ICBM during boost phase. After boost is completed, the targets are, or can be made, harder and thus require a greater fluence to destroy; and once the MIRVs are deployed they are not only much harder, but there are many more of them as targets. The defensive system can also be decoyed by false targets consisting of bright rockets and other hot sources simulating the missile exhaust.[4] And, if the history of MIRVs has anything to teach, it is that, faced with such a prospective defense under development and test, the Soviet Union could simply increase its arsenal of offensive missiles and warheads in order to maintain its deterrent. (At \$5 to \$10 million per warhead, the Soviets could buy a lot of warheads before equaling the DOD estimate in 1981 of \$500 billion for a space-based laser defense.)

In the final analysis, a very extensive and expensive constellation of chemical lasers predeployed in space appears to offer no credible prospect of forming an effective defensive layer against a large scale attack at the current high levels of the threat.[5]

"POP-UP SYSTEMS": GROUND-BASED X-RAY LASERS

In an effort to avoid most of the problems just described, the defense may choose not to predeploy in space, but to "pop-up" from the ground when alerted to an attack. The individual battle stations of such a system will have to be launched instantly as a missile payload. Thus, they must be substantially smaller and lighter than the infrared chemical lasers we have been describing, each one of which required about one shuttle load of fuel. Therefore, we must consider beam wavelengths much shorter than the micron range, since the wavelength of the light sets the scale size of the optics for a well-focused beam. Furthermore, a lighter and more compact energy source is required. This suggests that we consider x-ray wavelengths which are 100 to 1,000 times shorter than the IR wavgelengths of microns. The criteria of shorter wavelength and compact energy source both suggest an x-ray laser pumped by a nuclear explosive, which is a candidate system.

Therefore, we turn now to a consideration of a "pop-up" system consisting of x-ray lasers, driven by nuclear explosives, and mounted onto a missile that can itself be launched very rapidly upon receipt of information of an enemy attack. By itself, a nuclear explosion releases a very large amount of energy which is not focused, but which emerges in all directions. However, if a sufficiently large fraction of the energy from the nuclear explosion can be used to drive one or more lasers, and thus be focused into very highly collimated beams, it can cause severe impulsive damage to objects at very great distances. . . .

The kill mechanism in this case is impulsive damage due to ablative blow-off, caused by a very short intense pulse of incident energy, in contrast to the thermal heating by the chemical laser. The maximum kill range will depend on the gain that can be achieved in practice as well as the required kill fluence. This technology is still very immature,[6] but we shall assume here that there are no operational limits posed by limits in gain.

In considering the possibility of a practical "pop-up" system of this type, the most difficult and important operational issue to address is whether it can be deployed sufficiently rapidly even to attempt a boost-phase intercept. Modern ballistic missiles complete their powered flight, or boost phase, within three to five minutes after launch. At that point the remaining target becomes the post-boost vehicle consisting of the individual warheads and the "bus" on which they are mounted. The bus, which is considerably smaller than the booster, has its own internal guidance and power system for altering its path in order to drop off the individual warheads on their different trajectories. This means that a pop-up system, designed for boost-phase intercept, has itself only a few minutes available to be boosted to a high enough altitude above the atmosphere in order to be able to initiate an attack. In practice an x-ray laser can only operate at altitudes above 100 km. X-rays of 1 kev energy and lower are absorbed by the atmosphere at lower altitudes.[7] Thus a defensive x-ray laser would have to be launched literally within seconds of the launch of an initial enemy attack.

Furthermore, such a "pop-up" system would have to be based far off shore from continental U.S. soil, and near to Soviet territory. Otherwise, due to the curvature of the earth, it will be impossible for the x-ray laser beams to "see" the booster above the horizon before the end of burn. . . . The attacking missile is typical of current solid fuel ICBMs (and SLBMs) which complete boost in less than four minutes following launch and at altitudes below 250 km. The x-ray beams from the laser-interceptor must themselves always remain above the atmosphere. For example, if its distance from an attacking ICBM at an altitude of 200 km is as large as 3,000 km, a 1 kev x-ray laser itself must rise to an altitude above 350 km within the three minutes available to attack. This poses a severe requirement for a very high thrust booster for launching the laser defense. This defensive concept also requires that the command and control chain must operate almost instantaneously over great distances—and do so, after the first shots, in a heavily disturbed nuclear environment. Furthermore, the sensors to acquire, track, discriminate, and assess target damage must also operate accurately and reliably in a nuclear disturbed environment. Evidently such a system would have to be, essentially, entirely automated for quick response. This poses serious policy problems because the automated processes would have to be, essentially, entirely automated for quick response. This poses serious policy problems because the automated processes would necessarily include authorized release of nuclear weapons, as well as decisions as to whether and how to respond, depending on the intensity and tactics of the attack. For example, since an x-ray laser can fire only once, destroying itself in the act, should it be launched against a single attacking ICBM, or only against a suitably large barrage?

In addition to these formidable operational requirements, there are two technically available countermeasures by the offense that can *deny any possibility* of a pop-up x-ray laser defense.[8] The first countermeasure is simply to redesign the offense with new high-thrust "hot" missiles that complete their burn at altitudes below the top of the atmosphere. Unclassified studies[9] presented to the Fletcher panel calculate that the penalty in payload due to such rapid burn, lasting only about one minute, is no more than 10 to 15 percent. A second countermeasure is to alter the trajectory of the launch, depressing it so as to complete its burn below 100 km. Thus even if we assume that x-ray laser systems are successfully developed with sufficiently high gain—many orders of magnitude beyond current technology—to look promising for destroying boosters at long range, the offense can use the opacity of the atmosphere to defeat them with missiles of high thrust that complete their boost before they can be attacked.

HYBRID SYSTEM FOR BOOST-PHASE INTERCEPT

Other technologies and systems concepts have been proposed in an effort to escape the drawbacks of space-based and "pop-up" systems. One such concept that has been widely discussed is that of a system of ground-based lasers whose beams are aimed up to a small number of large relay mirrors in synchronous orbits at 36,000 km altitude. These relay mirrors at high altitudes then direct the beams to various mission mirrors, orbiting earth at lower altitudes from which they are redirected on to their targets. . . .

This hybrid system avoids three of the problems of a space-based laser defense: (1) fewer of its parts have to be protected from direct attack in space; (2) its ground-based lasers do not have to be replicated many times over in order to compensate for the large absentee ratio for lasers circulating in low earth orbits; and (3) it is not necessary to shuttle large amounts of fuel into orbit. It also avoids the very severe problem of time constraint for boost-phase intercept that is encountered by pop-up systems. However it faces several severe and unavoidable technical and operational challenges. First, the large focusing mirrors which are high value and crucial nodes of the system remain vulnerable in space. Also the directed light beams must travel very great distances, 36,000 km up and 36,000 km back from the relay mirrors in geosynchronous orbit. . . . Large optics and short wavelengths are necessary to reduce the diffraction and keep the energy focused on such a long path from laser to target. . . .

This concept necessarily relies on "active optics" in order to compensate for the effects of atmospheric turbulence that cause scattering and defocusing of the directed light beams (in a similar manner to which distant stars are seen as disks and jitter). "Active optics" means the following: a weak laser beam from space shines to ground and its beam spread is analyzed as a measure of local atmospheric turbulence, which is then compensated by use of deformable focusing mirrors for transmitting the beam from the ground-based laser. This technology, although still immature, has been progressing rapidly and, in principle, can achieve the goal of transmitting highly focused beams through the atmosphere.[10] In addition to atmospheric compensation there is the problem of weather, and in particular of cloud cover absorbing the laser energy. This requires replicating the ground-based lasers at widely distributed sites in order to have a high probability that an adequate number are free of cloud cover; or of basing the lasers high near mountain tops above the clouds. . . .

Even assuming that the technical goals are achieved, there still remains the operational problem of the vulnerability of the few large relay, and the mission, mirrors in space. They and the ground-based laser stations are reminiscent of the large phased-array radars of the earlier generation of ABM systems at the time of SALT I which proved to be their "Achilles heel." It has yet to be specified or understood how the small number of large and delicate mirrors in space, and of ground-based installations, can be protected with confidence.

OTHER CONCEPTS FOR BOOST-PHASE INTERCEPT

Another, somewhat more exotic, concept is that of using particle beams for directed energy weapons. Electrically neutral matter (atomic beams in particular) can travel large distances without being deflected by the earth's magnetic field, and is effective in depositing its energy within targets for destroying them. This is a very immature technology, however, much less advanced than the laser beams we have considered, and very little can be said about the practicality of orbiting operationally effective accelerators in space.[11] Large accelerators in space would of course be vulnerable to direct attack, as are any space-based systems. Like laser stations they would be more fragile to attack as well as more expensive than their targets—the ICBMs.

Directed energy weapons that are sources of high power microwaves have also been mentioned among the concepts for strategic defense. They too are in a very early stage in which the basic physics is still being studied, particularly with regard to how high a power can be achieved and how well it can be focused. It is too early to offer even educated guesses about their potential effectiveness, particularly against countermeasures, including shielding the targets against their radiation.

Finally, we mention the possibility of a boost-phase defensive layer that relies on material interceptors such as small missiles or pellet screens, launched from a constellation of space-based battle stations. Such "high frontier" proposals have been advanced as potentially being ready for deployment sooner than the more exotic directed energy beams.

Destruction of the target is achieved by the kinetic energy impinging on the booster when it encounters a high velocity interceptor or a cloud of matter in the form of debris or pellets. However, such schemes have been generally judged as ineffective for boost-phase intercept on grounds of time constraints, countermeasures, and vulnerability.[12]

MID-COURSE INTERCEPT AND BATTLE MANAGEMENT

The concept of a defense-in-depth envisages one or two layers operating during the mid-course phase, which for ICBMs lasts twenty to twenty-five minutes following the completion of the booster burn and prior to reentry of the warheads into the atmosphere. During the first few minutes of midcourse the post-boost vehicles will be targets before and while they are dispensing the individual warheads. Thereafter the surviving warheads are, individually, the targets. Although the time constraints are less severe, there are other factors that increase the difficulties of mid-course intercept. The post-boost vehicles are generally more difficult to destroy than are the boosters, since they are much smaller and harder to track; also they can be designed to be harder and to release the MIRVs very rapidly. The warheads are much smaller and harder still since they must withstand extreme stresses due to deceleration and due to heating up from atmospheric friction as they slam back into the top of the atmosphere. They are also far more numerous. In addition each missile may dispense hundreds of light decoys which follow the same paths in the absence of friction above the atmosphere as do the warheads.

While is it true that the capacity to analyze and transmit data has increased greatly in recent years, so has the size and sophistication of the offense—as well as its ability to confuse the defense. The offense can, for example, resort simply to anti-simulation to confuse the sensors and stress, if not saturate, the data-handling capacity of the defense. Antisimulation is the technique of making warheads look like decoys which can be dispensed in very much larger numbers with little weight penalty. One means to do this is to enclose the warheads in balloons with several thin metal-coated layers so that all balloons have the same appearance, whether or not there is a warhead inside. Additional severe difficulties can be caused by precursor detonations of nuclear weapons. The infrared radiation from the air heated by high-altitude nuclear explosions creates a severe background—known as "red out"—against which the sensors of a proposed mid-course ABM layer must operate and "see" the warhead.

As described in Defense Department documents,[13] the different layers of a defensive system would operate semiautonomously with their own sensors and data processing, as well as weapons and rules of engagement. As part of the overall battle management—i.e., monitoring, allocating the available defensive systems, assessing the results of the attack, and refiring if necessary—data would also be passed to successive layers in the defense. Input data from the sensors must be organized and filtered to see which objects can be discarded and which are candidates for further analysis—leading to tracking, attacking, and assessing damage. An effective boost-phase intercept that clears away close to 90 percent of the threat is thus very important in making the battle management and data-handling problems more tractable, and hence in achieving an effective strategic defense.[14]

No viable concept has yet been demonstrated or devised for a highly effective mid-course defense against a massive threat of many thousands of warheads plus many times more decoys.[15] The critical needs include not only a battle management software that far exceeds anything accomplished so far in complexity and difficulty,[16] but also the ability to protect all the critical space-based components, including many sensors, against enemy attack, whether from space mines, debris clouds, direct-ascent antisatellite weapons, or directed energy weapons (lasers) on ground or in space. Furthermore, to contribute to a mid-course defensive layer, these critical elements must survive throughout the entire time of the engagement up to final atmospheric reentry of the attacking warheads.

The directed energy systems described earlier for boost-phase intercept (chemical lasers based in space, or "pop-up" ground-based x-ray lasers) are also candidates for a mid-course defense. Although they would no longer face the severe time constraint of a boost-phase intercept, they face the operational problems we have just described. The entire system—including intelligence, communications, and surveillance satellites and the optical and directed high energy components, whether on ground, in low-earth orbit, or at synchronous altitude—must survive and operate in a hostile environment for many minutes in order to engage the threat. Moreover, each individual warhead—as well as the many additional decoys—will have to be attacked, and the warheads are generally much harder targets requiring a substantially larger kill fluence or impulse. Therefore, the overall energy requirements are greatly increased beyond the severe requirements already established in our earlier illustrations of boost-phase intercept.

TERMINAL DEFENSE

The terminal layer of the defense takes advantage of the atmosphere to slow down and strip away the lighter decoys accompanying the warheads in free space during mid-flight.

The requirements for a terminal defense of hardened military targets such as missile silos and command posts are much simpler and more readily achievable than for a strategic nationwide defense. Intercept can be made successfully much nearer to a target that is itself both small and hardened to withstand very high levels of overpressure. In addition, the goal of such a hard site defense is not to destroy all incoming warheads, but only enough of them to cause the attacker to expend more of his force than he destroys.

Improved technologies in recent years have enhanced the prospects for a cost-effective hard site defense that operates standing alone without prior layers of the defense. Important advances include interceptors that achieve much higher accelerations; improved accuracy that raises the possibility of nonnuclear kill; and sensors that can discriminate warheads from decoys at higher altitudes. Whether a hard site defense of a missile silo will, in reality, exact an "entry price" of two or three, or as many as six or seven attacking warheads per hardened target, is sensitive to many quantitative assumptions. The point to emphasize, however, is that hard site defense, whatever its potential and genuine merits, is very different from a goal of a nationwide defense designed to render nuclear weapons "impotent and obsolete." As such, it should be debated on its own merits.

The requirements of a terminal layer of a strategic defense of the nation are much more severe than for hard site defense since the urban-industrial targets are much larger and more vulnerable, and have much higher value. Standing alone, a terminal defense offers no prospect of defending the nation against a massive attack. This conclusion was reached during the earlier ABM debates of 1969-70, and the new technologies have added little to alter it. If, however, a terminal defense operates behind effective boost-phase and mid-course defensive layers which remove all but a few percent of the attack, the conclusion may be different. In particular, with improved sensors and interceptors, the defense may engage the incoming warheads at higher altitudes and contribute to limiting damage to the targets being defended. A terminal defense may thus limit damage as the final tier of a partially effective defense-in-depth.

OVERLAP WITH OTHER FORMS OF STRATEGIC DEFENSE

The ABM Treaty attempted to deal with the problem of "SAM upgrade" or, more generally, the problem that air defense systems or antitactical ballistic missile systems, or their components, might have some potential capability against strategic missiles. Since that time, new forms of the "SAM upgrade" problem have emerged as a result of technical advances. The sophistication of tactical aircraft and of strategic bomber armaments (now including air-launched cruise missiles or ALCMs), of land- or sea-based cruise missiles, of intermediate-range missiles (such as SS-20s and Pershing IIs), and of tactical missiles have continued to increase. Efforts to defend against aircraft and cruise missiles have led to modern generations of air defenses with improved radars, computers, and high-acceleration interceptors with growing potential to defend against these shorter range missiles. Moreover, intermediate-range ballistic missiles on 1,000 to 2,000 mile trajectories generally fly at lower speeds than longer range strategic missiles. This increases the time available for the defense to attack them in the terminal phase. Work is underway both in the Soviet Union and the United States to try to exploit this possibility of theatre, non-strategic ABM. Ways of updating the ABM Treaty to take account of this new form of the "SAM upgrade" problem will have to be addressed in future reviews of the Treaty.

ANTISATELLITE TECHNOLOGY (ASAT) AND DEFENSE VS. DEFENSE

ASAT is a much simpler technical problem than ABM defenses that operate above the atmosphere (exoatmospheric ABM), since the targets are softer, fewer, predictable both in their position and time, easier to discriminate, not easily replaced, and have communication and control links from earth that can be attacked. There is no question about the technical feasibility of ASAT systems that will be effective against satellites in low-earth orbit in the near future. Extending ASAT effectiveness to synchronous orbit altitudes of 36,000 km and higher will be a technical challenge, but presents no fundamental problems.

The significance of ASAT for strategic defense lies in the threat it poses against the space platforms of the ABM, in particular against the warning, acquisition, and battle management sensors. On the other hand, the significance of the Strategic Defense Initiative for ASAT is that it will spur technical developments that, inevitably, will be threatening to the critical communication and early warning satellite links on which a ballistic missile defense must rely. This presents an unavoidable dilemma: ASAT threatens ABM, but ABM developments contribute to ASAT.

More generally, ABM deployments will pose threats to each others' defensive systems, and in particular to the space-based components. This introduces the prospect of defense as an adjunct of a first strike. For example, a pop-up x-ray laser system launched as part of an attack can contribute to the overall advantage of a first strike by contributing to the suppression of both the defense and the retaliatory strike.

TECHNICAL SUMMARY

There have been major technological advances in recent years, but we do not now know how to build an effective nationwide strategic defense against ballistic missiles. This is true whether the goal is to transcend deterrence with a nearly leakproof defense or to enhance it with an effective but partial defense. It is true against the current Soviet threat—and there is no present prospect of achieving such a defense against an unlimited offensive threat that can overwhelm (i.e., more MIRVs and warheads); evade (i.e., fast burning "hot" boosters and cruise missiles whose flight paths lie entirely within the atmosphere); or directly attack the defense. As Dr. Richard DeLauer, Under Secretary of Defense for Research and Engineering, said to reporters on May 17, 1983, "With unconstrained proliferation, no defensive system will work."[17] Many years, if not decades, of research are required before we can begin to proceed from imaginative concepts, crude ideas, and estimates to educated guesses. If the system is to meet the President's stated goal of rendering nuclear weapons "impotent and obsolete," not only must it work to almost 100 percent perfection, managing an enormous task of battle management in very short times, but it must do this the very first time that it is used. No realistic shakedown tests are conceivable, especially in the nuclear environment the system will encounter in a real engagement. . . .

NOTES

1. Although specific system details are nonexistent and some component concepts may be classified, this is not an issue that need be, or should be, obscured behind an allegation of secrecy. Two studies of defensive technology have appeared recently: Ashton B. Carter, *Directed Energy Missile Defense in Space*, Background Paper

prepared for the Office of Technology Assessment of the Congress of the United States, April 1984; Union of Concerned Scientists, *Space-Based Missile Defense* (Cambridge: UCS, March 1984).

2. *Defense Against Ballistic Missiles: An Assessment of Technologies and Policy Implications* (Washington, D.C.: U.S. Department of Defense, March 6, 1984), p. 29.

3. As stated by General Lamberson in his testimony on March 23, 1983: "It is much easier to kill a satellite than it is a strategic aircraft, and doing that is much easier than killing a ballistic missile." *Strategic and Theatre Nuclear Forces*, Hearings before the Committee on Armed Services: Department of Defense Authorization for Appropriations for Fiscal Year 1984 (March-May 1983), U.S. Senate, 98th Congress, First Session (Washington, D.C.: USGPO, 1983), p. 2647.

4. Such rockets would have to appear like the ICBMs themselves, but would be much less expensive since they would carry neither warheads, MIRVs, buses, nor accurate guidance systems; nor would they have to be launched from underground silos.

5. In testimony, on May 2, 1983, to the Senate Armed Services Committee, Edward Teller, a leading proponent of a strong strategic defense, dismissed the practicability of such a system as follows: "I believe we should not deploy weapons in space, and in this sense to talk about starwars is a most inappropriate description of what the main question is. To put objects into space is expensive . . . infrared lasers, the presently known chemical lasers, do not seem to me to fulfill the basic requirement of a good defense, and that is that the defense must be considerably less expensive, must require considerably less effort than the offsetting effort in offense." *Strategic and Theatre Nuclear Forces*, Hearings before the Committee on Armed Services, op. cit., p. 2898.

6. It is reasonable to assume that a comparable level of fluence is required to destroy a booster by impulsive kill as by thermo-mechanical damage as discussed in the analysis of the chemical lasers. In order to deliver $20kJ/cm^2$ to a range of 1,500 km, the brightness of an x-ray laser will have to be increased by a factor of 10,000 beyond the goal reportedly recommended for demonstration in 1988 by the Fletcher committee.

7. The minimum altitude is even higher for lower energy x-rays since the absorption coefficient increases by a factor of 2^3 for each decrease by a factor of 2^3 in x-ray energy. The minimum altitude can be raised even higher by nuclear precursor explosions at high altitudes that are properly designed to heat the top of the atmosphere, thereby causing it to expand and rise.

8. These countermeasures also deny the possibility of basing x-ray lasers in space for boost-phase intercepts.

9. Briefing on "Short Burn Time ICBM Characteristics and Considerations," to the Defensive Technologies Study Team by Martin Marietta Denver Aerospace, with supporting backup analyses, July 20, 1983.

10. In his speech to the Council on Foreign Relations in Washington, D.C., Dr. George Keyworth, the President's Science Advisor, claimed that "we've also seen very recent advances that permit us to compensate for atmospheric break-up of laser beams." Dr. George Keyworth, *Reassessing Strategic Defense* (Washington, D.C.: Council on Foreign Relations, February 15, 1984), p. 12.

11. To quote from General Lamberson's testimony of March 23, 1983, to the Senate Armed Services Committee: "Particle beam technology is currently the least mature of the directed energy technology efforts." See *Strategic and Theatre Nuclear Forces*, Hearings before the Committee on Armed Forces, op. cit., p. 2653.

12. This view was expressed in response to questioning by Dr. Robert Cooper, Director of DARPA during his testimony to the Senate Armed Services Committee on May 2, 1983. He indicated that such "high frontier" concepts do not provide a cost effective potential for ballistic missile defense and could be countered at relatively low cost by the offense. We can illustrate their problems by considering the constraints on delivering the interceptors from their space-based platforms against the rising missiles before booster burn-out. Assuming a 200 second burn time for the booster and a typical closing speed of 10 km/sec (7 km/sec is orbital speed for low earth orbits), the maximum interceptor range is 2,000 km. Thus the absentee ratio for such a system will be high, comparable to what we saw earlier in our analysis of space-based chemical lasers. Furthermore, since each interceptor can attack only one booster, no fewer than 25,000 interceptor rockets will have to be launched into space on many hundreds of battle stations. The weight of each rocket will be typically several or more tens of kilograms as required to propel a projectile whose weight, including its homing sensors and divert rockets for final maneuver to impact with its target, will be several kilograms or more. This leads to a total system weight well in excess of 1,000 tons that has to be lifted into space. If the offense counters such a deployment with shorter burn times, the required size of the defensive tier would increase further. Finally these large space platforms share the vulnerability of all extensive space-based systems to direct enemy attack. See *Strategic and Theatre Nuclear Forces*, Hearings before the Committee on Armed Services, op. cit., p. 2891. For the most complete description of the "high frontier" concept, see Lt. Gen. Daniel O. Graham, *High Frontier* (Washington, D.C.; 1982).

13. See, for example, *Defense Against Ballistic Missiles: An Assessment of Technologies and Policy Implications*, op. cit.

14. In its summary of the Fletcher report, AWST describes the mid-course sensor constellation in a layered defense as consisting of 100 satellites, each weighing 20,000 kg for discrimination, precision tracking, and target designation. See Robinson, "Study Urges Exploiting of Technologies," op. cit., p. 50.

15. The following exchange during the Senate Hearings on May 2, 1983, between Senator Warner and the Director of DARPA, Robert Cooper, emphasizes the importance of the battle management problems. See *Strategic and Theatre Nuclear Forces*, Hearings before the Committee on Armed Services, op. cit., p. 2892.

Senator Warner: What in your view is the single greatest factor limiting our actions in the field of space-based ballistic missile defense? Is it financial resources or technological uncertainty?

Dr. Cooper: I think basically it is the technological uncertainty that we face in this general area. I think the single thing that we have not focused attention on in the past, which may represent the most stressing technological problem, is the complexity of any comprehensive battle that we would have to wage against a large-scale strategic missile attack.

It is the battle management problem, if you want to characterize it that way. Currently we have no way of understanding or dealing with the problems of battle management in a ballistic missile attack ranging upward of many thousands of launches in a short period of time.

This is the problem that we would face in the projected threat environment that the Soviets could project against us.

16. The first conclusion of the Battle Management, Communications, and Data Processing panel of the Fletcher Committee Report (vol. 5) was: "Specifying,

generating, testing, and maintaining the software for a battle management system will be a task that far exceeds in complexity and difficulty any that has yet been accomplished in the production of civil or military software systems."

17. Richard Halloran, "Higher Budget Foreseen for Advanced Missiles," *New York Times*, May 18, 1983, p. 11.

CHAPTER 10

Is SDI
Technically Feasible?

Harold Brown

* * *

Are the objectives of SDI technically feasible?

The answer will depend primarily on what specific objectives strategic defenses ultimately seek to achieve—protection of population, of missile silos, of other military targets. Within that context, the answer will further depend on the capabilities of the technologies and on the potential countermeasures and counter-countermeasures of each side.

This article will assess the prospects for the various defensive technologies for both the near term (10 to 15 years) and the longer term. . . . It will also make tentative judgments on the technical feasibility of various SDI objectives, though definitive answers are not yet possible. The political desirability of SDI is a separate question, not addressed here.

Finally, in considering the prospects for the various SDI technologies, it is important to remember how long it takes to move from technological development through full-scale engineering to deployment. That time is governed by the budgetary and legislative process, as well as by the state of technology.

- After the technology is proven out, full-scale engineering development of a moderately complex system will typically take five to eight years. . . .
- The course of deployment . . . takes five to seven years after completion of engineering development.
- Thus, if proven technology exists now, it will take 10 to 15 years before a new system employing the technology could be substantially deployed.
- If the technology needs to be further developed, even though the phenomena exist and are well understood, the time for that technology development will have to be added to such a period.

Excerpted by permission of Foreign Affairs, Volume 64, No. 3 (American and the World 1985). Copyright (1986) by the Council on Foreign Relations, Inc.

II

What kinds of technologies could be embodied in defenses against ballistic missiles that could begin deployment before or about the year 2000?

Terminal hard point defenses (e.g., defending ICBMs), using hardened ground-based radars and interceptor rockets, would require about ten years between a decision to deploy and having a significant force; the time to completion of deployment would approach 15 years from decision. The necessary technology exists now, and some subsystems have already been partially developed. . . . Such a system would include an interceptor like the Spartan missile aimed at reentry vehicles (RVs) outside the atmosphere, and another, rather like the Sprint missile, for intercepting RVs that have already entered the atmosphere.

Present designs of both missiles would require the use of nuclear warheads. Alternatively, non-nuclear versions could be developed using terminal homing devices in the interceptor. There is some question about how heavy a conventional warhead (and therefore the interceptor missile) would need to be in order to provide the high probability of destroying the incoming RV and missile warhead; it depends on how close to the reentry vehicle the terminal guidance could bring the interceptor. If a non-nuclear interceptor is chosen, this would lengthen by at least a few years the time to a substantial deployed capability.

An additional optical sensor, the Airborne Optical Adjunct (AOA), which would track reentry vehicles by detecting their infrared emissions or viewing them with visible light, could also be included at about the same time as a non-nuclear warhead.[1] Such a capability is feasible technologically and likely to be helpful in discrimination during or shortly before the offensive missile's reentry, but the technology would need some additional development.

Over the next 10 to 15 years it also appears technologically feasible to develop the components of a system using *space-based kinetic-energy weapons*. These chemically propelled rockets would intercept the offensive missile during its boost phase and destroy the target by impact or by detonation of an exploding warhead. The chemical rockets would be similar in nature to air-to-air missiles, but steered with reaction jets rather than aerodynamic surfaces. The targets could be designated to the interceptors by laser or radar tracks, provided by a set of tracking and fire-control satellites orbiting at a higher altitude than the satellites from which the interceptors would be fired. Short-range laser designation of ground or airborne targets exists, but the accuracies required for ICBM tracking would require significant additional technological development, as would imaging and processing the infrared data, and looking close to the horizon.

The interceptors would home onto the target, guided by their own passive observation of the infrared emissions from the target missile or by receiving reflections from the target of radar signals emitted from satellites (semiactive radar homing). Such a system, however, must find a way to direct the killer rocket to the actual ICBM booster rather than to its plume (exhaust), which emits the infrared signal. While presumably this can be done, it will add complexity. . . . Several years of additional technical development could significantly decrease the weight of the intercept rocket for a given kill probability. That approach is indicated because the weight determines a significant part of the total system cost. The cost of putting payloads in orbit with either the present shuttle or expendable boosters is thousands of dollars per pound. To reduce those costs to an acceptable level, a new "super" shuttle would probably have to be developed. This would involve a ten-year development process and a delay in deployment of a space-based kinetic-energy system.

Missile boosters in the upper atmosphere and in space can be detected, tracked and attacked through the infrared emissions of the missiles' exhaust plumes while their propulsion stages are burning. . . . Fast-burning boosters would effectively negate such a defense system.

Nevertheless, the technology for a space-based boost-phase intercept system of some capability, using kinetic-energy weapons, could be ready for a decision as early as 1990–92 to initiate full-scale engineering development, with a significant deployment able to begin some time between 1995 and 2000. Soon after the year 2000 there could thus be deployed a space-based kinetic-energy kill system along with a high-altitude and low-altitude terminal defense. These would constitute three layers of a possible multilayered defense, the purpose of which would be to compound modest kill probabilities in each defensive layer so as to produce a high overall kill probability.

III

For the period five to ten years beyond 1995–2000, more elaborate space- and ground-based technologies *may* be feasible, with a corresponding period of deployment beginning some time between 2000 and 2010. Increased uncertainty, however, naturally attaches the further out we look.

Among the less uncertain of these later technologies are *space-based directed-energy weapons* such as neutral particle beams and chemical lasers.

- A *neutral particle beam* (NPB) would be made up of atomic particles, accelerated to a high speed in charged form by electric fields in an accelerator, then steered and pointed by a magnet, and then neutralized so that it will not be deflected by the earth's magnetic field.
- A *chemical laser* uses the energy created by chemical reactions[2] to create a highly focused, intense, highly ordered ("coherent") beam of infrared light, directed by a mirror.

As a measure of their status, both of these technologies could well be used toward the early end of the period 2000–10 for antisatellite purposes, which are less demanding than the antiballistic missile task. Demonstrations of the capability to kill an individual satellite by such means—most likely on cooperative targets—could be made still earlier, but these would not represent an operational military system.

Neutral particle beams are, in their present state of development, much brighter than any existing laser in terms of energy into a given solid (cone) angle. Today they produce particles of energy corresponding to acceleration by a few million volts of electric field (and could in the future be improved to 100 million "electron-volt" energies). Protecting ballistic missiles from such high-energy NPBs would require much heavier shielding than would protection from lasers. During the next 10 or 15 years, however, it is unlikely that NPB technology will be able to put more than ten percent of the primary energy into the particle beam itself. Such low efficiency means that a space-based NPB would probably require a nuclear power source, development of which would delay the possible deployment of a system.

In addition to the usual target acquisition and tracking problems, a defense based on neutral particle beams has several other critical tasks. The magnet necessary to point the beam before its neutralization is likely to be heavy—and expensive—to put into space. The tasks of developing an ion source capable of operation over some minutes and of achieving the necessary pointing accuracy will be difficult. Even more difficult is tracking the beam, since it gives off almost no signal in space. Finally, the system will need to find ways to detect the effect on the target, through nuclear emanations from it, because at the full range of a successful NPB attack, the target would not be physically destroyed. Even where NPBs cannot be used to kill targets, however, they might ultimately prove useful in discriminating among them, because the nuclear emanations from an object hit by an NPB would depend on the object's weight.

For chemical lasers several technological problems still need to be solved. One is getting high enough power while maintaining a low enough beam divergence. Another is the very large weight of chemical reactants required for providing the energy. A third is the feasibility of the large optical systems required. There are, however, some promising technologies under development for chemical and other lasers. Among them are: various phase-compensation techniques to improve the quality and stability of the beam; phase-locking separate lasers together to increase the overall brightness; using adaptive optics (rapid adjustment of segments of a mirror), both to compensate for atmospheric dispersion for ground-based lasers and to ease the problems of creating large aperture mirrors for space-based ones; and phased arrays of lasers to increase intensity and to steer them more rapidly through a small angle, so as to move quickly from target to target. But some of these technologies have yet to reach full demonstration of the physical principles involved, and all are still far from being developed.

IV

Less technologically developed, and therefore more suitable for consideration of full-scale deployment beginning 20–25 years from now, is the use of ground-based *excimer* and *free-electron lasers* (FEL)[3] to be used with mirrors in space as components of a system for boost-phase intercept. Both are now many orders of magnitude away from achieving the intensity necessary for the required lethality, the free-electron laser further away than the excimer laser, at present. But the free-electron laser's device weight is lighter and its efficiency greater (and thus, its fuel weight lighter) than that of the excimer laser. The FEL might perhaps therefore be deployable in space. But the weights of these lasers and of their energy supplies more probably would require either to be ground based. The laser wavelength for both would allow the beams to penetrate the atmosphere, if the atmospheric distortions problem is solved. Thus both seem more suitable for ground deployment along with mirrors in space. Other problems for the ground-based lasers are the large optics required, both on the ground and for the synchronous-altitude steering mirrors, and obtaining the same high power in each of a long series of repetitive pulses.

These two systems might also be suitable for "active" discrimination—also called "interactive" or "perturbing"—in the mid-course phase of a strategic defense. That is, they could impart energy or momentum to very large numbers of objects in mid-course being tracked by some of the more established technologies already discussed. The resulting changes in the objects being tracked, or in their trajectory, could offer some limited opportunities for discrimination of reentry vehicles from decoys and debris.

Significant technological disagreement exists about the potential of ground-based lasers (free-electron or excimer) versus space-based chemical lasers. . . .

Chemical lasers are more proven technologically than excimer or free-electron lasers, but many experts have dismissed their potential use because of the difficulties in designing an effective system. Chemical lasers (space-based because their wavelengths will not penetrate the atmosphere) could be of some use against ballistic missiles now deployed. They could well be severely inadequate, however, against the offensive systems (with, for example, fast-burn missiles and other countermeasures) that could be in place during the first decade of the next century, when a significant defensive laser deployment could be made. Surely such countermeasures would be put in place if defense lasers were deployed. And in light of the large weight of chemical fuel that would have to be deployed in space, the chemical laser system at present seems to fall into the category of technically feasible but ineffective as a system. New optical developments such as phased arrays and phase conjugation are now being investigated, however. These might be able to improve the brightness and stability of chemical lasers—and increase their lethal range—to the point where they would have some systems effectiveness even against a responsive threat.

X-ray lasers powered by nuclear explosions are still further off than the other types of lasers, although they seem to offer some interesting distant possibilities. X-ray lasers would have wider beam angles and higher power per unit solid angle than optical ones. This would make them suitable for destroying clouds of objects or for actively discriminating heavy objects among them, and thus effective against such countermeasures as balloons and decoys. Proof of the most basic principle has been established, in that bomb-driven X-ray lasing has been demonstrated to be possible. But there is doubt as to what intensity has been achieved; it is in any event far less than necessary for use in active discrimination, let alone target kill. Demonstration of the physics of a possible weapon is at least five (more likely ten) years off. Weaponization would involve another five or more years, and only thereafter could its incorporation into a full-scale engineering development of a defensive system begin.

Rail guns, which accelerate objects to very high speed electromagnetically, may also have promise. But they are almost as far off as X-ray lasers. . . .

While many uncertainties exist as to future laser technologies for strategic defense, all laser systems would be vulnerable to other lasers. In general, the rules of the competition are that ground-based lasers will defeat space-based ones, larger ones will defeat smaller ones, and bomb-driven X-ray lasers looking up through the fringes of the atmosphere will defeat the same sort of X-ray lasers looking down into the fringes of the atmosphere. . . .

As to time scale, when one is talking about time scales for deployment 25 or more years from now, corresponding to technologies whose full demonstration is more than ten years away, one really cannot know what the time scale will be to reach substantial deployment. The accompanying chart summarizes the time scales for these various systems. For the space-based systems, the pop-up systems and those with mirrors in space, lengthy technology development periods will be required. Depending on how that development is carried out, it may be possible to defer collision with the provisions of the ABM treaty until early in the process of full-scale engineering development. The calendar times differ for each technology, as shown in Figure 1.

V

A successful strategic defense would require not only kill mechanics but also a *battle management system* involving sophisticated *command, control and communications* (C³). Estimates for the total number of lines of code of software required range from 10 million to 100 million. . . .

One problem would be with errors in the codes themselves. While this would not be trivial, it could be dealt with in part through automated software production and through artificial intelligence. The most fundamental problems for battle management and C³ are: the establishment of appropriate rules of engagement; the probability of conceptual as well as mechanical error in the creation of the software, and the possibility of redundancy to compensate for it; the need to change portions of the software as new elements are introduced into the system without having the changes compromise the working of the rest of the software; and, most of all, the ability to check out the system, so as to make sure there are no conceptual errors in the software in such matters as handing over tracks of the offensive

FIGURE 1

Technology	1985	1990	1995	2000	2005	2010	2015	2020

Ground-Based Missiles:

Low-altitude nuclear

Non-nuclear

High-altitude

Mid-course intercept

Space-Based:

Kinetic-energy weapons

Neutral particle beam

Chemical laser

Ground-Based with Mirrors in Space:

Excimer laser

Free-electron laser

Space-Based or Pop-up X-ray Laser (bomb-driven)

Technology Development ☐   Full-Scale Engineering Development ▨   Deployment ■

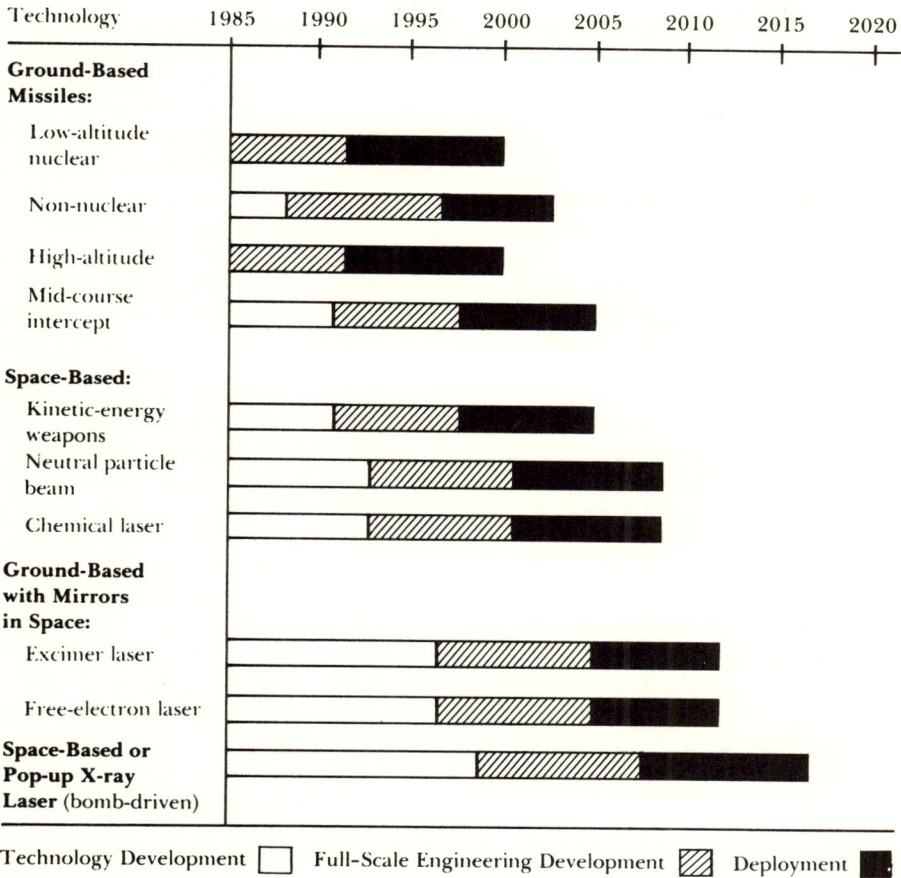

missiles, transferring automated decisions from one node of the system to another, avoiding loops in the logical sequence, and so forth.

How could such capabilities be tested? Can on-orbit testing be used? Such problems are just beginning to be addressed, and it will take a long time before conclusions can be drawn even as to what the state of this particular technology is compared with what is needed.

VI

In terms of future defensive technologies, what potential defense systems are technically feasible?

It is technologically feasible to create a *terminal defense* overlay of hard ICBM silos, deployed so that the missiles are moved among multiple silos and so that their position at any one time is unknown to the attacker. Such a defense overlay can, by preferential defense—that is, defending only the occupied silos—provide a cost-exchange ratio favorable to the defense because the attacker must attack all silos. The same is probably true of defense of moderately hardened mobile missile systems by a terminal defense of corresponding mobility and hardness. In the case of hard-silo defense, a single layer of defense by endoatmospheric ground-based interceptors would suffice. For mobile hardened missiles, a two-tier ground-based system would probably be needed.

Modified ground-based defenses using similar technologies could protect some other military targets, for example command and control centers. The exchange ratio at the margin will vary widely, however, among classes of such targets according to their nature (hardness, area and mobility), their number and their cost. Such defenses could also be deployed for a thin protection of some urban-industrial areas, though they must be recognized as protecting such targets, if at all, only against attacks that are both limited in size and not responsive (i.e., not modified to take account of the defenses). Terminal defenses for these categories would use two-tier ground-based interceptors, and until the early 21st century would need to carry nuclear warheads in at least the exoatmospheric long-range tier. The defenses would be accompanied by space-based early warning and tracking sensors, and by airborne optical sensors to aid in the discrimination task during the terminal phase.

Advanced versions of infrared sensors deployed near or above geosynchronous orbit (an altitude of 20,000 miles) will be needed for attack warning and assessment in any defensive system, even if no boost-phase intercept is attempted. Infrared or other sensors in lower orbits (at altitudes of hundreds of miles) would also be useful to all layers of a ballistic missile defense system for tracking and discrimination. But the sensors must be able to survive. This suggests that they be provided with some self-defense, which in turn could be the first step toward boost-phase intercept.

As to weapons, kinetic-energy rockets based in space are technologically feasible. But an ICBM using a fast-burn booster clearly defeats them, and space-based defenses are vulnerable to defense suppression. Estimates of the exchange ratio for a *boost-phase intercept* defense layer based on kinetic-energy kill range from as low as two to one adverse to the defense at the margin (assuming unresponsive offensive threats and including sunk costs for the offense) to more realistic estimates, assuming responsive offenses, of five or ten to one. Defense suppression would probably further shift the ratio in favor of the offense.

Space-based chemical lasers seem feasible in technological terms but more questionable in practical systems terms. Though likely to be faster in response than kinetic-energy weapons, they still will not be a match for fast-burn boosters of offensive missiles. They will, moreover, be vulnerable to defense suppression systems based on other space-based lasers, and also vulnerable to ground-based lasers and direct-ascent antisatellite weapons. Ground-based lasers, whether free-electron or excimer lasers, are interesting future technologies and may be more effective than chemical lasers, but it is too soon to know.

It should be noted that even though fast-burn missiles could thwart a boost-phase intercept, this still leaves the possibility of a *post-boost tier* or layer in an SDI system. The deployment by the offense of warheads and decoys cannot occur until later in the trajectory than the boost phase, at a higher altitude in order to avoid atmospheric drag. But the technology for post-boost intecept capabilities is likely to be difficult to achieve, because it will require electronic examination of images (pictures), using ordinary or infrared light, to distinguish among various components: the burned-out upper stage of the missile, the post-boost vehicle, and the various objects released from it. These requirements, the countermeasures, and the potential technological capabilities for a post-boost layer of defense are just beginning to be considered.

Which technologies would be useful in the next tier, in *mid-course intercept*, is still less understood. Presumably the defense would want to use the same kill methods (kinetic-energy and directed-energy weapons) for intercepts as in the other tiers. This has the advantage of allowing some of the absentee satellites[4] to come into play because of the longer time period involved in mid-course flight of a missile. Discrimination among possibly colossal numbers of objects would, however, be a daunting problem. There are ideas about how to address it, but no confidence in any of them; that is why there is a drive toward consideration of "active" discrimination, which would impart energy to the objects in the threat cloud in order to be able to distinguish among them by observing the effect on their behavior. Thus, mid-course intercept is unlikely to play any role in a deployed system until well after the turn of the century.

Through all of these considerations is entwined a serious problem for space-based ABMs: however effective space-based systems may be against ballistic missiles, they would appear to be more effective in suppressing defenses. And direct-ascent antisatellite systems or ground-based lasers may be still more effective than space-based systems in this latter role.

In sum, given the state of present and foreseeable technology, a boost-phase or post-boost phase intercept tier is not a realistic prospect in the face of likely offensive countermeasures and the vulnerability of those tiers to defense suppression. It will also exhibit unfavorable relative marginal costs as a contributor to defense of population at any reasonably high level of protection. These judgments apply to any system beginning deployment at least for the next 20 years, and probably considerably beyond then.

There are interesting new technologies, however, that leave open the possibility that our estimates of the offense-defense balance might change after that time, especially if some of these technologies prove to have some mid-course discrimination and intercept capability, as well as some boost-phase effectiveness. Such a shift is very unlikely, but strategic thinking should include the possibility that it might take place in terms of deployed systems some decades into the next century. . . .

To sum up, the near-term prospects for ballistic missile defense capabilities are reasonably well known. Technically, they appear cost-effective for defense of some kinds of strategic retaliatory forces. For defense of populations against a responsive threat, they look poor through the year 2010 and beyond. The prognosis for the longer term for this latter objective in the contest between defense and offense is less certain. It still looks questionable, at best, for the defense, because of some fundamental problems of geometry and geography, and the physics of offensive countermeasures and defense suppression in their contest with defense.

NOTES

1. Development or testing of AOA beyond the technology platform stage, as a component of an ABM system, even of a fixed ground-based ABM system, would appear to violate the ABM treaty because the AOA is itself a mobile component.

2. For example, the chemical combination of hydrogen and fluorine. If the population of the resulting excited molecules outnumbers that of the lowest-energy ("ground") state, stimulation of emission of light of the frequency corresponding to the energy difference occurs, resulting in an intense coherent beam.

3. Excimer lasers use "excited" (higher-energy) states of molecules including a rare gas (e.g., argon) and a halogen (e.g., iodine). These excited states are quasi-stable, while the unexcited ("ground") states are not populated, because the rare gases are not chemically active in their lowest-energy states. Free-electron lasers use the effect of oscillating electromagnetic fields on electron beams to cause the electrons to emit phase-coherent (laser) radiation.

4. Satellites in nonsynchronous orbit trace out a path over the earth whose pattern and timing depends on their altitude and velocity. Absentee satellites are those whose position in their orbits, at the time when the attacking missiles are launched, puts them over parts of the earth that are distant from the offensive launch sites.

CHAPTER 11

The Strategic Defense Initiative: Defensive Technologies Study

James C. Fletcher

. . . The Study Team identified a long-term, technically feasible research and development plan. The goal of the study was to provide the basis for selecting the technology paths to follow when a specific defensive strategy is chosen. At the same time, near-term demonstrations of some system components were identified that could provide options for early deployment and meaningful levels of effectiveness against constrained threats. The plan also incorporates ideas for enhancing the defense of NATO and other allies.

The study reviewed, evaluated, and placed priorities on the technological issues underlying the ballistic missile defense of the United States and its allies. Also reviewed was a set of strategic defense system concepts and supporting technologies in various states of development. In addition, the study considered system concepts where technological attributes were not preeminent, for example, concepts constrained by fiscal considerations. The study did not consider defenses against threats other than ballistic missiles, such as bombers and cruise missiles or conventional forces; these issues are dealt with in other Department of Defense studies.

The Defensive Technologies Study Team identified a research and development program to allow knowledgeable decisions on whether, several years from now, to begin an engineering validation phase that, in turn, could lead to an effective defensive capability in the 21st century. Similarly, intermediate deployments could be feasible that would provide meaningful levels of defense, especially against constrained threats.

The Defensive Technologies Study concluded that

Excerpted from "The Strategic Defense Initiative: Defensive Technologies Study," Department of Defense, March 1984.

- Powerful new technologies are becoming available that justify a major technology development effort offering future technical options to implement a defensive strategy. . . .
- The most effective systems have multiple layers, or tiers.
- Survivability of the system components is a critical issue whose resolution requires a combination of technologies and tactics that remain to be worked out.
- Significant demonstrations of developing technologies for critical ballistic missile defense functions can be performed over the next 10 years that will provide visible evidence of progress in developing the technical capabilities required of an effective in-depth defense system.

ADVANCES IN DEFENSIVE TECHNOLOGIES

The ballistic missile threat has increased significantly over the past 20 years, so an appropriate question is: "What has happened to justify another evaluation of ballistic missile defense as a basis for a major change in strategy?" Advances in defensive technologies warrant such a reevaluation.

Two decades ago there were no reliable approaches to the problem of boost-phase intercept; however, multiple approaches now exist based on directed energy concepts such as particle beams and lasers and kinetic-energy target destruction mechanisms.

Intercept in midcourse was difficult 20 years ago because of no credible concepts for decoy discrimination, the intercept cost, and the collateral effects of nuclear weapons used for the interceptor warheads. Today, multispectral sensing of discriminants with laser imaging and millimeter-wave radar, birth-to-death tracking, and direct-impact projectiles that have promise as inexpensive interceptors appear to eliminate the difficulties of midcourse intercept.

In the 1960s an inability to discriminate penetration aids at high altitudes and limited interceptor performance resulted in very small defended areas for each terminal site and required an unacceptably high number of interceptors for effective defense. Now, technological advances may offer ways to discriminate among incoming objects and to allow intercepts at high altitudes. When these improvements are coupled with the potential for boost-phase and midcourse intercepts to disrupt pattern attacks, the effectiveness of terminal defenses is significantly increased.

Likewise, 1960s technology in computer hardware and software and signal processing was incapable of supporting battle management of the multitiered defense. Because of technological advances, the needed command, control, and communications facilities in all likelihood will be realized.

Several new technologies and concepts emerged from the work of the Defensive Technologies Study Team that, considered with those already well known, illustrate how far defensive technology has progressed over the past two decades. For example, throughout the phases of a ballistic missile trajectory, there are many observables, and by using both active and passive sensors, a selection of them can be measured. That is, it is likely that discrimination can be done between a warhead and a decoy or debris as threat objects proceed toward their targets. . . . Although any one sensor can be defeated, it is very difficult to defeat several operating simultaneously. . . .

THE THREAT

A variety of potential threats were considered, ranging from an attack with fewer than 100 ballistic missiles and a few hundred warheads to a simultaneous launch attack with more than 3,000 missiles and over 30,000 warheads. The Study Team selected a defense-in-depth approach because of the stress imposed by a maximum, unconstrained ballistic missile offense. The critical technologies highlighted later are best understood in the context of this threat. . . .

THE BALLISTIC MISSILE DEFENSE ENVIRONMENT

. . . There are four phases of a typical ballistic missile trajectory. . . . First, there is a boost phase when the first- and second-stage engines are burning and offering intense, highly specific observables. A post-boost, or bus deployment, phase occurs next, during which multiple warheads and penetration aids are released from a post-boost vehicle. Then, there is a midcourse phase when warheads and penetration aids travel on ballistic trajectories above the atmosphere. Finally, there is a terminal phase in which the warheads and penetration aids reenter the atmosphere and are affected by atmospheric drag.

A ballistic missile defense capable of engaging the target all along its flight path must perform certain key functions:

- *Rapid and reliable warning of an attack and initiation of the engagement.* This requires global, fulltime surveillance of ballistic missile launch areas to detect an attack and define its destination and intensity, to determine likely targeted areas, and to provide data for handoff to boost-phase intercept and post-boost vehicle tracking systems.
- *Efficient intercept and destruction of the booster and post-boost vehicle.* The defense must be capable of dealing with attacks ranging from a few tens of missiles to a massive, simultaneous launch. In attacking post-boost vehicles, the defense prefers to attack as early as possible to minimize the number of penetration aids deployed.
- *Efficient discrimination through bulk filtering of lightweight penetration aids.* The price to the offense in mass, volume, and investment for credible decoys should be high.
- *Enduring birth-to-death tracking of all threatening objects.* . . .
- *Low-cost target intercept and destruction in midcourse.* There should be recognition of the assigned target in the midst of a large array of penetration

aids and debris. The cost to the defense for interceptors should be less than the cost to the offense for warheads.
- High endoatmospheric terminal intercept and destruction. . . .
- Battle management, communications, and data processing. . . .

It is generally accepted, on the basis of many years of ballistic missile defense studies and associated experiments, that an efficient defense against a high-level threat would be a multitiered defense-in-depth requiring all the capabilities listed above. For each tier there will be leakage, that is, threat objects that have not been intercepted and hence move on to the next phase. For example, three tiers, each of which allows 10 percent leakage, yielding an overall leakage of 0.1 percent, are likely to be less costly than a single layer that is 99.9 percent effective. In addition, a multitiered defense is the optimum counter to structured attacks: any given offense response affects only one phase. . . . Because the terminal defense of a large area requires many interceptor launch sites, the defense is vulnerable to saturation tactics.

It is desirable, therefore, to complement the terminal defense with area defenses that intercept at long ranges. Such a complement is found in a system for exoatmospheric intercepts in the midcourse phase.

Intercept outside the atmosphere requires the defense to cope with decoys designed to attract interceptors and exhaust the defending force prematurely. . . . Intercept before midcourse is attractive because starting the defense at midcourse accepts the potential of a large increase in targets from multiple independently targeted reentry vehicle and decoy deployment.

The ability to respond effectively to an unconstrained threat is strongly dependent on the viability of a boost-phase intercept system. For every booster destroyed, the number of objects to be identified and sorted out by the remaining elements of a layered ballistic missile defense system is reduced significantly. Because each future booster could be capable of deploying tens of reentry vehicles and hundreds of decoys, the leverage, or the advantage gained by the defense, may be 100 to 1 or more. A boost-phase system is itself constrained by the relatively short engagement times and the potentially large number of targets. . . .

That phase of flight in which post-boost vehicle operations occur is a transition from boost phase to midcourse. In this phase the leverage gained by the defense decreases with time as decoys and reentry vehicles are deployed. On the other hand, the post-boost phase offers additional time for intercept by boost-phase weapons, and above all an opportunity to discriminate between warheads and deception objects as they are deployed. . . .

SURVEILLANCE, ACQUISITION, AND TRACKING

Just as there are many tiers to the overall ballistic missile defense system, there can be more than one tier in each of the phases. These space-based surveillance, acquisition, and tracking components perform different tasks because the nature of a structured attack changes as the threat objects proceed along their trajectories. . . .

The midcourse sensors must be able to discriminate between the threatening reentry vehicles that have survived through the post-boost deployment phase and nonthreatening objects such as decoys and debris. . . .

Space-based, passive infrared sensors could provide a way to meet these requirements. They could permit long-range detection of cold bodies against the space background, rejection of simple lightweight objects, and birth-to-death tracking of designated objects. . . .

INTERCEPT AND TARGET DESTRUCTION

A variety of mechanisms, including directed energy, can destroy a target at any point along its trajectory. The study identified several promising ones. An excimer laser, for example, can be configured to produce a single giant pulse that delivers a resulting shock wave to a target. The shock causes structural collapse. A continuous-wave or repetitively pulsed laser delivers radiant thermal energy to the target. Contact is maintained until a hole is burned through the target or the temperature of the entire target is raised to a damaging level. Examples included in this category are free-electron lasers, chemical lasers (hydrogen fluoride or deuterium fluoride), and repetitively pulsed excimer lasers. Another way to destroy a target is with a neutral-particle beam, which deposits sufficient energy within a target to destroy its internal components. Guns and missiles destroy their targets through kinetic-energy impact. Here, homing projectiles are propelled by chemical rockets or by hypervelocity guns, such as the electromagnetic gun based on the idea of an open solenoid. . . .

Ultimately, data must be distributed to authorities external to the defense system to infer or sense the development of hostilities, to determine a defense condition level and take appropriate actions with respect to weapons release, to assist in inferring the attacker's intent, and to evaluate the effectiveness of the defense and anticipate damage.

Developing hardware will not be as difficult as developing appropriate software. Very large (order of 10 million lines of code) software that operates reliably, safely, and predictably will have to be deployed. Fault-tolerant, high-performance computing will be necessary. It must be maintenance-free for 10 years, radiation-hardened, able to withstand single-event upset, and designed to degrade gracefully. . . .

SURVIVABILITY

Survivability is potentially a serious problem for the space-based components. The most likely threats to the components of a defense system are direct-ascent antisatellite weapons; ground- or air-based lasers; orbital antisatellites, both conventional and directed energy; space mines; and fragment clouds. . . .

Ideally, the defense system should be designed to withstand an attack meant to saturate the system. . . .

OFFENSIVE RESPONSES

In all considerations of offense versus defense, there is a continuing dynamic interaction. Each action can stimulate a countermeasure. . . . It should be noted that each projected response involves a trade-off; for example, hardening of booster rockets means a reduced payload or range.

CRITICAL TECHNOLOGIES

The Defensive Technologies Study Team concentrated on critical technologies, that is, the technologies basic to the longest lead-time items. . . . The concern was primarily with the technologies that are paramount—the concepts whose feasibility will determine whether an effective defense is possible.

There are several critical technological issues that will probably require research programs of 10 to 20 years.

- *Boost and post-boost phases.* As mentioned earlier, the ability to effectively respond to an unconstrained threat is strongly dependent on meeting it appropriately during the boost and bus deployment, or post-boost phases. This is especially important for a responsive threat.
- *Threat clouds.* Large threat clouds—that is, dense concentrations of reentry vehicles, decoys, and debris in great numbers—must be identified and sorted out during the midcourse phase and high reentry.
- *Survivability.* It will be necessary to develop a combination of tactics and mechanisms ensuring the survival of the system's space-based components.
- *Interceptors.* By having inexpensive interceptors in the midcourse phase and in early reentry, intercept can be economical enough to permit attacks on threat objects that cannot be discriminated.
- *Battle Management.* Tools are needed for developing battle-management software.

The study also identified 5- to 10-year research programs dealing with other issues. One category is space logistics. In order of priority within this category, it is desirable to have (1) a heavy-lift launch vehicle for space-based platforms of up to 100 metric tons, (2) a capability to service the space components, (3) a capability to make available, on orbit, sufficient materials for space-component shielding against attack, and (4) an ability to transfer items from one orbit to another. In addition to these items, multimegawatt power sources for space applications would be required.

NEAR-TERM DEMONSTRATIONS AND DEPLOYMENTS

An informed decision on system development cannot be made before the end of the decade, but there may be reasons for near-term feasibility demonstrations that could be developed into elements of a total ballistic missile defense system. Unlike the boost and post-boost phases, the trade-offs between competing technological approaches for the midcourse and terminal phases are relatively well understood. Although we cannot yet pick detailed designs for the major components of the midcourse and terminal-phase defenses, the best generic approaches are known and the set of competing technologies is narrow. A number of near-term demonstrations could be done before the end of the decade that typify technological milestones. Such demonstrations could include, among others, a space-based acquisition, tracking, and pointing experiment; a megawatt-class, visible-light, ground-based laser demonstration; an airborne optical adjunct demonstration; and a high-speed, endoatmospheric, nonnuclear interceptor missile demonstration.

In the next five years there are decision points that will affect the technologies available by 1990. Between 1990 and 2000 the United States may decide to provide increasing protection for its allies and itself by deploying portions of the complete four-phase system. Such deployments might be evolutionary, leading to the final, low-leakage system.

The members of the Defensive Technologies Study Team finished their work with a sense of optimism. The technological challenges of a strategic defense initiative are great but not insurmountable. By pursuing the long-term, technically feasible research and development plan identified by the Study Team and presented in this report, the United States will reach that point where knowledgeable decisions concerning an engineering validation phase can be made with confidence. The scientific community may indeed give the United States "the means of rendering" the ballistic missile threat "impotent and obsolete."

CHAPTER 12

SDI:
The Last, Best Hope

Edward Teller

* * *

THE UMBRELLA

Shortly before 6 p.m. on March 23, 1983, I arrived at the White House. I had received a cryptic message a few days earlier that I should be there for dinner, but it was only just before dinner that I learned of the approximate content of the president's speech.

"Isn't it better to save human lives than to avenge them?"—this was the line in the speech that I shall never forget. In a few words it summarized all my worries and all my hopes. Minutes after the president finished his talk, Secretary of State George Shultz, with whom I worked for many years, asked me: Could we stop 99.9 percent of the incoming missiles?

The question is most important. How complete can the defense be? No amount of war damage is "acceptable": War must be avoided. Defense happens to be the best deterrent for aggression.

The answer is no. A 99.9 percent defense cannot be attained soon. It may not ever be attained. Even if it is attained, it will not be attained with complete certainty.

But defense does not need to be a tight umbrella. It suffices if it makes the success of an attack uncertain.

A defense of America and the free world that is not complete but that makes the outcome of an attack dubious would have great persuasive power to deter aggression. To my mind, and, I believe, to anyone's mind in a democracy, a third world war is not winnable. I believe that for a Soviet leader it is winnable only if it results in complete world domination—in the annihilation of the United States. That is why even an imperfect and uncertain defense would be an excellent deterrent. Mikhail Gorbachev could

---

Excerpted by permission of the author from *Insight*, October 28, 1985.

not count on an absolute victory. The grizzly bears in the Kremlin don't like to take chances.

THE DEFENSES

1. Rocket vs. Rocket

In 1984, a short-range, inexpensive U.S. device, assisted by radar, tracked and intercepted an approaching rocket at an altitude of 100 miles with remarkable accuracy. This accuracy was not even necessary because the defensive missile opened up like an umbrella to cover a considerable area. The velocity of the two approaching objects was so great that the incoming rocket would have been destroyed if any portion of the umbrella had touched it.

Against a massive attack, this defense would not suffice. . . .

These rocket interceptors could provide some protection before the end of this decade. But this system is inadequate as the only national protection against a large-scale attack.

2. Short-Range Laser Defenses

Progress in directed-energy weapons was the main reason why, six years ago, I became confident about the feasibility of defense. Today, a limited but significant success of defense is not a mere possibility; it is a high probability. . . .

To destroy satellites in space is the least difficult military application of lasers. This is an important reason why predeployed battle stations in space are not apt to survive. But ground-based lasers may play an important role in providing direct defense against short-range missiles (fired from 100 miles away) in less than 10 years.

Lasers of the necessary energy are being developed rapidly and effectively. . . .

However, the beam of a ground-based laser must be transmitted through the atmosphere without distorting its favorable regular properties. Turbulent air causes density changes that deflect light. . . .

Such diffusion of a laser beam makes the beam far less effective. The problem is not insoluble. Astronomers have recognized for years that irregularities in atmospheric density can be compensated for if one replaces big curved mirrors with an array of many small mirrors, which can be oriented in a fraction of a second to eliminate the twinkling. Rapid progress in solving this problem in a practical manner is currently being made.

Unfortunately, clouds stop laser beams, though high-intensity light can bore a hole through thin clouds for the requisite short time. Still, duplication of laser installations at various locations will be needed to ensure that at least one of the beams will get through. This, incidentally, is also an insurance against attempts on the part of the attacker to put the defense out of action.

While short-range missile defense is important to the United States as a protection against missiles launched from off-shore submarines, such a defense system is most interesting for our allies.

Laser defense does not use any nuclear devices, is not connected with any deployment of battle stations or anything else in space, and does not violate any treaties because such defenses are purely tactical. Therefore, laser defense against short-range missiles is likely to be the defense first deployed.

3. Long-Range Laser Defense

The short-range lasers described above would not be effective against missiles whose range is much more than 100 miles. But the range of these lasers can be extended by the use of mirrors. Such mirrors would be deployed on the ground but would be popped up out of the atmosphere at the time of an enemy attack. The longer the distance, the higher the needed pop-up and the greater the difficulty.

The mirrors required become smaller and easier to handle as the wavelength of the defense laser becomes shorter. Short-wavelength lasers are also more efficient in destroying enemy rockets. . . . If a usable X-ray laser can be produced, we will have made an immense step forward in our ability to defend ourselves. These lasers would be the most effective; they are also the most difficult to develop.

It should be noted that X-ray lasers will not penetrate the atmosphere. They and their power sources, would have to be lofted outside the atmosphere. The only power source that can be popped up is a nuclear explosive. Powering an X-ray laser with a nuclear device would have no serious effect on the Earth's surface.

4. The Electron Beam

One radically different directed-energy weapon probably capable of destroying missiles in flight is an electron beam device. This instrument could be used in the moderately high atmosphere, though not outside the atmosphere. . . .

5. Defense in Space

Reagan did not speak of stars, space, satellites—only about defense. There are advantages to deploying defense in space. There are also great disadvantages. The deployed defenses can be attacked over many months, even years. Space defense may not be impossible, but it is certainly difficult. I believe that in one case we should try to use space deployment: to protect our space-based monitoring systems.

A rocket launch is accompanied by the sudden, characteristic appearance of a powerful infrared radiation burst. This can be easily detected from space, for instance from a synchronous satellite. Even now, we have such observation satellites.

It is possible but difficult to protect these early-warning systems. We can try to make them "hard" or replaceable. We can also try to deploy inconspicuous "sleeping detectors" which will unfold and become active only when the functioning detector is incapacitated. These sleepers in turn may be protected by decoys.

All this can be done. Whether it can be done cheaply enough to be really effective is an open question. It will help to make the detecting system as simple as possible.

Detectors in space may, in turn, be backed up by Earth-based radars. These radars will be highly effective against attack. If the radars work at long wavelengths, ionization in the high layers of the atmosphere will confine the propagation of these waves to the neighborhood of the Earth's surface so that the radar will follow the curvature of the Earth over long distances. This is called over-the-horizon (OTH) radar. The OTH radar will locate the launching of a rocket over any distance, because the launching emits plenty of electromagnetic waves of long wavelength. Thus we can know when to pop up our defense systems, particularly in the case of a massive attack. However, the problem of detection needs much more attention.

Space deployment—"star wars," if you please—has many purposes. The Soviets are working on it. We must be aware of the possibilities. But we should not follow suit until we know that the system is effective and survivable. The most hopeful, though not mandatory, approach is to use stations in space for early warning.

Not battle stations, but observation posts!

COMPUTERS

Computers are important for defense. Indeed, without computers, defense against a massive attack could hardly work. Computers may make it possible to keep track of thousands of rockets and many more decoys. Does this mean that vital decisions must be turned over to computers? When one understands the root of the problem, the answer becomes obvious.

One real danger of nuclear conflict is connected with the fact that the crisis may occur fast and it may be over—with a tragic ending—in practically no time. Decisions must be made in minutes or even seconds. Whom can one trust with fast decisions? I would not trust myself. I would not trust anyone. There is no perfect solution. We must be satisfied with an imperfect solution. After careful consideration, the best alternative seems to be the computer.

It has been claimed that the computer system that must be deployed is beyond our capabilities. In particular, to write a program that will function under battle conditions is an unprecedented challenge.

But anyone who gives up at this point has forgotten that a tenfold improvement in computer technology has occurred regularly in every decade since 1945.

Bibliography: Part Three

Brown, Harold. "Defensive Systems and the Strategic Debate," public lecture celebrating the fifteenth year of the California Seminar on International Security and Foreign Policy at the Beckman Auditorium, California Institute of Technology, in November 1984. Reprinted in *Essays on Strategy and Diplomacy*, No. 3. Claremont, Calif.: Keck Center for International Strategic Studies, 1985, pp. 16–32.

Drell, Sidney D., Philip J. Farley, and David Holloway. *The Reagan Strategic Defense Initiative: A Technical, Political, and Arms Control Assessment.* Stanford, Calif.: International Strategic Institute, 1984.

Fletcher, James C. "The Technologies for Ballistic Missile Defense." *Issues in Science and Technology* (Fall 1984):15–29.

Panofsky, Wolfgang K. H. "The Strategic Defense Initiative: Perception vs. Reality." *Physics Today* (June 1985):34–45.

Stone, Jeremy J. "The Four Faces of Star Wars: Anatomy of a Debate." Federation of Atomic Scientists *Public Interest Report* 38, no. 3 (March 1985):1–9.

Union of Concerned Scientists. *The Fallacy of Star Wars.* Cambridge: 1983.

U.S. Congress, Office of Technology Assessment. *Anti-Satellite Weapons, Countermeasures, and Arms Control.* Washington, D.C.: Government Printing Office, September 1985.

U.S. Congress, Office of Technology Assessment. *Directed Energy Missile Defense in Space—A Background Paper.* Prepared by Ashton B. Carter. Washington, D.C.: Government Printing Office, April 1984.

Yonas, Gerold. "Strategic Defense Initiative: The Politics and Science of Weapons in Space." *Physics Today* (June 1985):24–32.

PART FOUR

SDI AND U.S.-SOVIET RELATIONS

U.S.-Soviet relations will be affected by the many issues about which the two countries disagree. The extent to which the United States pursues SDI is one of those issues.

The public Soviet position on SDI is emphatically negative. The Soviet government has repeatedly said that no progress on strategic arms control can occur until the United States abandons SDI. In response, the United States has said (see editors' Introduction) that it will conduct SDI research within the limits of the ABM Treaty. U.S. policymakers have also added their belief that the Soviets will move from their position and come to accept a negotiated transition away from offensive nuclear deterrence to a reliance on defense. The Soviet position on SDI and on strategic arms control as a whole is covered in the selections by Soviet Communist party leader Mikhail Gorbachev and an expert on Soviet strategy, David Holloway.

There have been some signs of Soviet willingness to negotiate reductions in both sides' nuclear arsenals in Europe without prior agreement on SDI. Unfortunately, this willingness has been accompanied by a precondition unacceptable to the United States and its nuclear armed European allies, Britain and France. The Soviet government has said that negotiations on reducing nuclear arms in Europe may go forward only if the British and French agree to freeze their arsenals at their present size and the United States pledges not to transfer nuclear weapons or other technology to either European country. Because the British and French are on the verge of modernizing and drastically increasing the numbers and effectiveness of their arsenals, and because the British have opted to buy U.S. missiles for their new ballistic submarines, the Soviet offer has been flatly rejected.

SDI has been accompanied by a number of ambitious comprehensive arms control proposals from the Soviet and U.S. government. The Reagan administration was first into the arena with the new brand of proposal when it called for a 50 percent reduction in nuclear warheads and launchers. With the installation of Gorbachev the Soviet government announced a similar proposal, contingent as always on U.S. abandonment of SDI. On paper the two sides are remarkably close, since both propose to cut arsenals in half as a prelude to even more significant reductions. Although this is encouraging, it is discouraging to watch the two sides play at public diplomacy.

The history of arms control suggests that the present level of publicity means that serious progress is unlikely. Summaries of the latest U.S. views of SDI's effects on U.S.-Soviet relations are given in President Reagan's address to Congress after his return from the Geneva summit with General Secretary Gorbachev and the remarks by Special Presidential Adviser Paul Nitze.

CHAPTER 13

Nuclear Disarmament by the Year 2000

Mikhail S. Gorbachev

. . . The Soviet Union proposes that a step-by-step, consistent process of ridding the earth of nuclear weapons be implemented and completed within the next 15 years, before the end of this century.

. . . How does the Soviet Union envisage today in practical terms the process of reducing nuclear weapons, both delivery vehicles and warheads, up to their complete elimination? Our proposals on this subject can be summarized as follows.

Stage One. Within the next 5 to 8 years the USSR and the USA will reduce by one half the nuclear weapons that can reach each other's territory. As for the remaining delivery vehicles of this kind, each side will retain no more than 6,000 warheads.

It stands to reason that such a reduction is possible only if both the USSR and the USA renounce the development, testing and deployment of space strike weapons. As the Soviet Union has repeatedly warned, the development of space strike weapons will dash the hopes for a reduction of nuclear armaments on earth.

The first stage will include the adoption and implementation of a decision on the complete elimination of medium-range missiles of the USSR and the USA in the European zone—both ballistic and cruise missiles—as a first step towards ridding the European conflict of nuclear weapons.

At the same time the United States should undertake not to transfer its strategic and medium-range missiles to other countries, while Great Britain and France should pledge not to build up their respective nuclear arsenals.

The USSR and the USA should from the very beginning agree to stop all nuclear explosions and call upon other states to join in such a moratorium as soon as possible.

The reason why the first stage of nuclear disarmament should concern the Soviet Union and the United States is that it is they who should set

---

Excerpted from the *New York Times*, "Nuclear Disarmament by the Year 2000," February 5, 1986, p. 5.

an example for the other nuclear powers. We said that very frankly to President Reagan of the United States during our meeting in Geneva.

Stage Two. At this stage, which should start no later than 1990 and last for 5 to 7 years, the other nuclear powers will begin to join the process of nuclear disarmament. To start with, they would pledge to freeze all their nuclear arms and not to have them on the territories of other countries.

In this period the USSR and the USA will continue to carry out the reductions agreed upon during the first stage and also implement further measures aimed at eliminating their medium-range nuclear weapons and freezing their tactical nuclear systems.

Following the completion by the USSR and the USA of a 50 percent reduction of their respective armaments at the second stage, another radical step will be taken: All nuclear powers will eliminate their tactical nuclear weapons, i.e., weapons having a range (or radius of action) of up to 1,000 kilometres.

At this stage the Soviet-U.S. accord on the prohibition of space strike weapons would become multilateral, with the mandatory participation in it of major industrial powers.

All nuclear powers would stop nuclear tests.

There would be a ban on the development of nonnuclear weapons based on new physical principles, whose destructive power is close to that of nuclear arms. or other weapons of mass destruction.

Stage Three will begin no later than 1995. At this stage the elimination of all remaining nuclear weapons will be completed. By the end of 1999 there will be no nuclear weapons on earth. A universal accord will be drawn up that such weapons should never again come into being.

We envisage that special procedures will be worked out for the destruction of nuclear weapons as well as for the dismantling, re-equipment or scrapping of delivery vehicles. In the process, agreement will be reached on the number of weapons to be scrapped at each stage, the sites of their destruction, and so on.

Verification of the destruction or limitation of arms should be carried out both by national technical means and through on-site inspections. The USSR is ready to reach agreement on any other additional verification measures. . . .

II

Guided by the same approach and a desire to take another practical step within the context of the nuclear disarmament programme, the Soviet Union has adopted an important decision.

We are extending by three months our unilateral moratorium on all nuclear explosions, which expired on December 31, 1985. Such a moratorium will remain in force even longer if the United States for its part also stops nuclear tests. We propose once again to the United States that it join this initiative, the significance of which is evident to practically everyone in the world. . . .

I wish to say the following at the outset; Any references to verification as an obstacle to the establishment of a moratorium on nuclear explosions are totally groundless. We declare unequivocally that for us verification is not a problem. Should the United States agree to stop all nuclear explosions on a reciprocal basis, appropriate verification of compliance with the moratorium would be fully ensured by national technical means as well as with the help of international procedures, including on-site inspections when necessary. We invite the United States to reach agreement with us to this effect.

The USSR resolutely stands for making the moratorium a bilateral, and later, a multilateral measure. We are also in favour of resuming the tripartite negotiations, involving the USSR, the USA and Great Britain, on the complete and general prohibition of nuclear weapons tests. This could be done immediately, even this month. We are also prepared to begin without delay multilateral test-ban negotiations within the framework of the Geneva Conference on Disarmament, with all nuclear powers taking part.

Nonaligned countries have proposed that consultations be held with the aim of extending the 1963 Moscow Treaty Banning Nuclear Weapons Tests in the Atmosphere, in Outer Space and Under Water to cover also underground tests, whose ban is not envisaged in the Treaty. The Soviet Union agrees to this, too.

III

. . . In a few days the Soviet-American talks on nuclear and space arms will be resumed in Geneva. When we met with President Reagan last November in Geneva, we had a frank discussion on the whole range of problems which are the subject of those negotiations, namely on space, strategic offensive armaments and medium-range nuclear systems. It was agreed that the negotiations should be accelerated and this agreement must not remain a mere declaration.

The Soviet delegation in Geneva will be instructed to act in strict compliance with that agreement. We expect the same constructive approach from the U.S. side, above all on the question of space. Space must remain peaceful: strike weapons must not be deployed there. Neither must they be developed. And there must also be introduced very strict control, including the opening of relevant laboratories for inspection.

Mankind is at a crucial stage of the New Space age. And it is time to abandon the thinking of the stone age, when the chief concern was to have a bigger stick or a heavier stone. We are against weapons in space. Our material and intellectual capabilities make it possible for the Soviet Union to develop any weapon if we are compelled to do so. But we are fully aware of our responsibility to the present and future generations. It is our profound conviction that we should approach the third millennium not with the Star Wars programme, but with large-scale projects of peaceful space exploration by all mankind. We propose to start practical work in developing and implementing such projects. This is one of the most important ways of ensuring progress on our entire planet and establishing a reliable system of security for all.

To prevent the arms race from spreading to outer space means to remove the obstacle barring the way to drastic reductions in nuclear weapons. On the negotiating table in Geneva is a Soviet proposal to reduce by one half the corresponding nuclear arms of the Soviet Union and the United States, which would be an important step towards the complete elimination of nuclear weapons. To block all possibility of resolving the problem of space indicates a lack of desire to stop the arms race on earth. This should be stated in clear and straightforward terms. It is not by chance that the proponents of the nuclear arms race are also ardent supporters of the Star Wars programme. These are two sides of the same policy, hostile to the interests of people.

Let me turn to the European aspect of the nuclear problem. It is a matter of extreme concern that in defiance of reason and contrary to the national interests of the European peoples, American first-strike missiles continue to be deployed in certain Western European countries. This problem has been under discussion for many years now. Meanwhile, the security situation in Europe continues to deteriorate.

It is time to put an end to this course of events and cut this Gordian knot. The Soviet Union has long been proposing that Europe should be free of both medium-range and tactical nuclear weapons. This proposal remains valid. As a first radical step in this direction we now propose, as I have said, that even at the first stage of our programme all medium-range ballistic and cruise missiles of the USSR and the USA in the European zone should be eliminated. . . .

CHAPTER 14

The Strategic Defense Initiative and the Soviet Union

David Holloway

. . . None of the important questions that have been raised about the technical and operational feasibility of the SDI, or about its effect on U.S. security, the risk of nuclear war, and the prospects for arms control, can be answered without some consideration of the Soviet leaders' view of President Reagan's initiative and of their likely response to it.

DETERRENCE AND DEFENSE IN SOVIET POLICY

. . . Marshal V.D. Sokolovskii's *Military Strategy*, which was the most important study of strategy published during that period [published in the early 1960s], declared that "one of the cardinal problems for Soviet military strategy is the reliable defense of the rear from nuclear strikes."

Sokolovskii, who had been chief of the general staff from 1952 to 1960, acknowledged that "in contemporary conditions the means and methods of nuclear attack unquestionably prevail over the means and methods of defense against them."[1] Yet claims made by Soviet leaders in the early 1960s suggested that the Soviet Union had found a way of carrying out the mission of strategic defense. . . .

Soviet BMD policy in the early 1960s was rooted in an unwillingness to regard vulnerability to nuclear attack as an acceptable basis for Soviet security. . . .

Soviet military strategy assigned BMD an important role in the conduct of war. According to Sokolovskii, the National Air Defense Forces (which have responsibility for BMD) would have the primary role in protecting

Excerpted by permission of the author and *Daedalus*, Journal of the American Academy of Arts and Sciences, Weapons in Space, Vol. II: Implications for Security, Summer 1985, Cambridge, Massachusetts.

the country from nuclear strikes and in repelling the enemy's nuclear attack. . . .

In 1967 and 1968, as the Soviet leaders were preparing for the SALT negotiations, there were signs of a change in their thinking about BMD. There seemed to be disagreement in the high command about BMD's effectiveness. . . .

Alongside the growing doubts about the technical effectiveness of BMD came an increasing confidence in the deterrent power of the Soviet Union's offensive strategic forces, which were now approaching parity with those of the United States. . . . Marshal N.V. Ogarkov, the former chief of the general staff, has written that in the early 1960s the United States could count "to some extent" on the possibility of a disarming strike against the Soviet Union.[2] But by the late 1960s, the United States, in the Soviet view, could no longer do so.

The Soviet leaders acknowledged that each side was vulnerable to a devastating retaliatory strike if it attacked first. . . . Soviet policy at SALT was based on the recognition that the existing nuclear balance could be upset by the deployment of either offensive or defensive systems.

In May 1969, Maj. Gen. V.M. Zemskov, one of the leading Soviet military theorists, wrote in *Military Thought* that the nuclear balance of power could be disrupted if either country sharply increased its offensive forces, or deployed a highly effective BMD. If the United States tilted the balance in its favor, he wrote, the danger of nuclear war would grow.[3] Given this view of the strategic balance, it seems likely that the Soviet leaders' fear of an unconstrained BMD race with the technologically superior United States played some part in convincing them of the desirability of the ABM treaty. . . .

But this was not the only factor in the Soviet decision to sign the treaty. The Soviet leaders were aware that the deployment of BMD systems would stimulate further development of offensive forces. During the exploratory moves before SALT, the Soviet Union had asked that defensive and offensive systems be considered together. The preamble to the treaty notes that "effective measures to limit anti-ballistic missile systems would be a substantial factor in curbing the race in strategic offensive arms," and in September 1972, Marshal A.A. Grechko, the defense minister, claimed that the treaty would help prevent competition between strategic offensive and defensive weapons.[4]

Some of the arguments advanced against BMD in the Soviet Union were similar to those expressed in the contemporary American debate: BMD would not be effective against a large-scale attack by offensive missiles; BMD deployment would spur the other side into increasing its offensive forces; a BMD race might tilt the nuclear balance in the American favor, and this would increase the danger of war. . . .

The ABM treaty thus codified a situation in which the Soviet Union and the United States were equally vulnerable to a retaliatory strike, no matter who struck first. Soviet leaders have continued to recognize this mutual vulnerability. Marshal Ogarkov wrote in 1983 that as a result of the numbers and technical characteristics of the nuclear weapons on either side, the defending side would always retain so many nuclear weapons that in a retaliatory strike it would be able to inflict "unacceptable damage" on the aggressor.[5] And in words that echo the opening Soviet statement at SALT in November 1969, he added that "in contemporary conditions only suicides can wager on a first nuclear strike."

Although the Soviet leaders recognize mutual vulnerability to devastating retaliatory strikes as an objective condition, they do not regard nuclear war as impossible. At SALT, they showed concern about the danger of war occurring as a result of miscalculation, and about the possibility that a third nuclear power might provoke a world war. . . .

The Soviet leaders have also thought it prudent to prepare for nuclear war, in case it should occur. Even within the confines of the relationship of mutual vulnerability, Soviet military strategy still focuses on how to wage nuclear war and defeat the enemy. Soviet leaders say that their military doctrine is defensive in purpose, but Soviet military strategy sees the offensive as the primary form of military operation. In a war, Soviet forces would aim to seize the initiative and to inflict defeat on the enemy by means of decisive military actions. As Marshal Ogarkov put it:

We are speaking about being able not simply to defend oneself by opposing the aggressor with the appropriate passive means and methods of defense, but of inflicting on him destructive retaliatory blows and defeating the enemy utterly in any conditions of the situation as it develops.[6]

The Soviet leaders recognize the existence of mutual vulnerability to devastating retaliatory strikes, and at the same time feel it necessary to devise a military strategy for the conduct of nuclear war in case it should occur. BMD could, in principle, play a role in waging a nuclear war, and this element in Soviet thinking has led many Western observers to regard Soviet BMD activities since 1972 with suspicion, especially since the Soviet Union has continued to modernize its air defenses, and thus has not abandoned the idea of strategic defense as a whole.

SOVIET BMD ACTIVITIES SINCE 1972

. . . Since 1972, there has been virtually no discussion of BMD in the Soviet military press. But the Soviet Union has maintained a large and steady R&D effort on BMD technologies.

The Soviet Union is upgrading the Moscow BMD system by replacing the Galosh interceptor missiles with SH-04 and SH-08 nuclear-armed interceptors. The SH-04 is an exoatmospheric interceptor, like Galosh, and the SH-08 is a hypersonic endoatmospheric interceptor, like the American Sprint. New phased-array radars (the Pushkino radar) are being built to perform the engagement function. These activities are permitted by the ABM treaty, which limits the number of interceptors to one hundred, and forbids deployment at any other site. The upgraded Moscow system would be ineffective against a determined American strategic strike, but it could provide some defense against theater systems such as Pershing II, and against nuclear attacks by other powers; it would also provide some defense against accidental launches.

A recent CIA report has raised the specter of a Soviet breakout from the ABM treaty through the deployment of a nationwide BMD system or of extensive defenses for its ICBM fields.[7] The Soviet Union now has the SH-04 and SH-08 interceptor missiles and the new radars in production and, with its large missile and radar industries, could deploy them on an extensive scale. There is no conclusive proof that this is the Soviet intention, however, and it would take years rather than months to carry out a strategically significant deployment. The system would not be leakproof; it could be overwhelmed, and the radars would be vulnerable to attack. The United States could respond effectively, with relatively modest effort, by improving the penetration of its offensive systems.

The Soviet Union has also been doing extensive research into the use of directed energy for military purposes, and some of this work may be intended for BMD. Most estimates of the quality of Soviet directed energy research put it on a level with that in the United States. But in other technologies that are crucial for BMD, the evidence suggests that the United States enjoys a considerable advantage. According to the U.S. Department of Defense, the United States leads in: computers, optics, automated control, electro-optical sensors, propulsion, radar, software, telecommunications, and guidance systems.[8] There is little doubt that, with its more advanced technology, the United States could make more rapid progress than the Soviet Union towards the development of a space-based BMD system. The Soviet Union, on the other hand, could move more quickly to the deployment of a conventional BMD system for mid-course and terminal defense.

The modernization of Soviet air defenses to deal with cruise missiles and improved bombers has given them the ability to handle smaller radar cross-sections and shorter reaction times, and has thus made them more capable against ballistic missile reentry vehicles (RVs). The problem is most dramatically illustrated by the SA-12 air defense missile, which is reported to have been tested not only against aerodynamic systems, but also against ballistic missile RVs. It may have been designed for use against tactical and theater ballistic missiles, as well as against aerodynamic systems, and it may also have some capability against SLBM RVs. Developments in surface-to-air missile (SAM) technology have made the problem of surface-to-air-missile upgrade, which caused difficulties in the ABM treaty negotiations, even trickier. The treaty could be modified to cope with the way in which technological advances have blurred the distinction between air defense and BMD. This problem could also be addressed unilaterally by the United States if it deployed modest decoys and used existing technology to reduce RV radar cross sections.

A more specific issue of compliance is raised by the new radar near Krasnoyarsk, which appears to be similar to the early warning radars at

Pechora, Komsomol'sk-na-Amure, and Kiev. It is oriented outwards, towards the northeast, and could detect Trident SLBMs launched from the Bering Sea or the Gulf of Alaska. If this radar, which is not yet operational, is indeed an early-warning radar, it violates article VI.b of the treaty, which limits the deployment of ballistic missile early-warning radars to locations along the borders of the two countries and requires that they be oriented outwards. The significance of this radar for BMD is negligible because it is not accompanied by interceptor missiles and engagement radars of the Pushkino type, and would be vulnerable to destruction or blackout in a nuclear attack. But it does raise a serious issue of compliance with the treaty.

The Soviet BMD effort since 1972 appears to have had a number of purposes. It has sought to provide Moscow with some defense against accidental strikes or attacks by third nuclear powers. It has tried to develop defenses in those areas not covered by the treaty—against Pershing IIs, for example—and thus supplements Soviet defenses against bombers and cruise missiles. It has provided a hedge against United States breakout from the ABM treaty. It has also explored new technologies that might one day radically alter the balance between offense and defense. Whatever the reasons behind this effort, however, the arguments against BMD advanced by the Soviet Union in the late 1960s—concern about the effectiveness of BMD, the possibility of an arms race in both offensive and defensive systems from which the United States might emerge with an advantage, and the danger of war—still seem to hold sway. Soviet BMD activities since the ABM treaty do not necessarily imply a shift in attitude.

It is nonetheless prudent for the United States to monitor Soviet activities very carefully, and to question them in the Standing Consultative Commission if they are suspicious or ambiguous. It is also prudent for the United States to conduct research into penetration aids and BMD technologies in case the Soviet Union should decide to break out of the treaty. But current Soviet BMD activities do not justify the claim that the Soviet Union has already broken out of the treaty, or is intending to do so in the near future.

THE SOVIET ASSESSMENT OF THE SDI

The Soviet reaction to President Reagan's "Star Wars" speech of March 23, 1983, was quick in coming. In a statement issued four days later, General Secretary Andropov said that the defensive measures Reagan spoke of would seem defensive only to "someone not conversant with these matters."[9] The United States, said Andropov, would continue to develop its strategic offensive forces with the aim of acquiring a first-strike capability.

Under these conditions the intention to secure itself the possibility of destroying with the help of ABM defenses the corresponding strategic systems of the other side, that is of rendering it incapable of dealing a retaliatory strike, is a bid to disarm the Soviet Union in the face of the United States nuclear threat.

Andropov claimed that the attempt to build a BMD system would intensify the arms race. . . .

Andropov's response to Reagan's speech was hardly surprising. It was inevitable that the American goal of building an effective BMD should be seen by the Soviet leaders as, first of all, a threat to their ability to retaliate in the event of an American first strike. Both President Leonid Brezhnev and Defense Minister Dmitri Ustinov had claimed in 1982 that the Reagan administration was pursuing military superiority as part of its program to destroy socialism as a socio-economic system.[10] The MX ICBM, the Trident D-5 SLBM, the Pershing II, and the land-, sea-, and air-based cruise missile programs were all portrayed as part of a concerned effort to achieve superiority. The Soviet leaders apparently feared that even if these programs did not enable the United States to escape from the threat of retaliation, they might nonetheless give it a preemptive superiority, aimed at reducing the effectiveness of a Soviet retaliatory strike.[11]

Since this was already the official Soviet interpretation of United States policy, President Reagan's "Star Wars" speech was bound to be viewed as a new and dangerous stage in the drive for strategic superiority.

Andropov's response to Reagan's speech also expressed dismay at the implicit intention to abrogate the ABM treaty. Along with other agreements negotiated by the Soviet Union and the United States in the early 1970s, the ABM treaty embodied some measure of common understanding on how best to manage the strategic arms competition without precipitating nuclear war. Andropov chided Reagan for ignoring the link between offensive and defensive strategic weapons, and for failing to understand that BMD deployment would stimulate the competition in offensive systems. Other Soviet commentators have warned that BMD would make war more likely because it would create the illusion of invulnerability, and thus increase the temptation to strike first. It is ironic that these are precisely the arguments that Americans used in the late 1960s to persuade the Soviet Union that BMD was destabilizing. . . .

Although Soviet spokesmen have been vocal about the SDI, they have been reticent about the purposes of their own BMD activities, and this contrast, though not unusual in Soviet practice, has aroused suspicion in the West. It is true that a great deal of what they have said has been designed to influence Western public opinion. Nevertheless, the Soviet leaders' assessment of the SDI is quite consistent with the view of the strategic relationship that they have expressed since the late 1960s, when they acquired an assured retaliatory capability. Since then they have regarded this capability as a basic condition of Soviet security, and seem to fear that it may now be threatened by United States plans to develop and deploy BMD.

THE SOVIET MILITARY RESPONSE TO THE SDI

. . . Three broad options are open to the Soviet Union, either separately or in combination: it can upgrade its retaliatory forces, it can develop weapons that could destroy the space-based BMD system, or it can deploy its own BMD system. Each of these responses needs to be assessed in terms of its technical feasibility, economic cost, and contribution to Soviet military policy.

Offensive Missiles

The Soviet leaders regard their ability to inflict devastating retaliatory strikes on the United States as one of the basic conditions of Soviet security in the present circumstances. Their most obvious response to the SDI, therefore, would be to upgrade their offensive forces in order to ensure that they can penetrate, evade, or overwhelm the defense. They could increase the number of their offensive ballistic missiles, thereby complicating the task of the defense, and diversify their forces by deploying nuclear weapons in space or by making greater use of bombers and cruise missiles, which would not be vulnerable to BMD.

In order to complicate boost-phase interception, which brings the greatest gain to the defense, the Soviet Union could shield its launchers with reflective or ablative materials, thus raising the power requirement for the defense's kill mechanisms. It could also shorten the boost phase by developing fast-burn ICBMs. A payload penalty of about 10 to 30 percent might have to be paid in order to reduce the boost phase from three hundred to sixty seconds, but the gain would be an enormous increase in the difficulty of boost-phase interception.

President Reagan's science adviser, Dr. George A. Keyworth II, has written that "if the fast-burn booster is possible at all, it is probably three to five generations away from those ICBMs the Soviets already have in the works."[12] On the other hand, the Defensive Technologies Study Team, which reported to the Department of Defense in the summer of 1983, concluded that the Soviet Union could develop a fast-burn booster within fifteen years without a crash program. This seems a more realistic estimate than Keyworth's. It is true that the Soviet Union has had problems in mastering solid-fuel propulsion, but its latest ICBMs (the SS-24 and SS-25) and SLBM (the SS-N-20) are all solid-fuel missiles. Moreover, the SH-08 hypersonic endoatmospheric BMD interceptor missile employs technology similar to that needed for a fast-burn ICBM. This indicates that the Soviet Union could develop fast-burn ICBMs before the SDI reaches the stage of deployment.

Keyworth has also argued that boost-phase defense would cause the Soviet Union "to completely change directions with a fifteen-year investment in 75 percent" of its strategic forces. But even if the Soviet Union were to deploy the new missiles at the same rate as it deployed its ICBMs between 1977 and 1982, it could replace its existing force with fast-burn boosters within ten years. According to CIA estimates, between 1967 and 1977, the Strategic Rocket Forces absorbed no more than 10 percent of Soviet military outlays. (Figures for 1977–1982 are not available, but there is no reason to suppose that the proportion exceeded 10 percent of Soviet outlays in those years either.[13]) It therefore seems that the Soviet Union could reequip its

ICBM force with fast-burn boosters without devoting more than 10 percent of its military outlays to this program.

The Soviet Union could also take measures to overload or confuse the mid-course and terminal phases of the defense by deploying more RVs on its existing launchers. The Soviet ICBM force, with its large throw-weight, is particularly well-suited to countermeasures of this kind. The SS-18 ICBM, for example, which is limited to ten RVs under the provisions of SALT II, could carry up to thirty. Decoys could also be deployed, with possibly even hundreds of decoys to one RV. This would present the defense with the formidable problem of identifying the real RVs in mid-course where there is no atmospheric drag to sort them out from the decoys.

Dr. Keyworth has argued that an American BMD system would force the Soviet Union to move away from its reliance on ICBMs and to eschew any thought of a first strike. In a speech in February 1983, he claimed that the Soviet leaders, when confronted with mounting evidence that the ICBM is no longer an effective first-strike weapon, will shift their strategic resources to other weapons systems.[14] But it is not evident that the Soviet leaders will react in this way. Far from considering offensive ballistic missiles obsolete, they are likely to see them as one of the chief means for ensuring penetration and saturation of the defense, and might wish to exploit all their ballistic missile throw-weight for countermeasures.

Dr. Keyworth has also written that "the most immediate argument in favor of developing active defenses" is that "they remove the preemptive option both for the Soviet Union and the United States."[15] It is true that BMD would increase the uncertainties associated with a first strike and might lessen its effectiveness. But it would not necessarily make such a strike less likely. Soviet strategic writings have shown an interest in preemption, in striking first when it is believed that the other side is about to attack—and this is the case to which Keyworth refers in his article. The issue to be weighed in deciding on preemption is not the absolute advantage to be gained from striking first, but rather the balance of advantage between striking first and striking second. If the United States had BMD and could destroy some significant part of the Soviet offensive forces in a first strike, then the Soviet incentive to preempt in a crisis might well be increased, not diminished, by the fear of having to launch a weakened retaliatory strike against the defense.

It seems unlikely, therefore, that the SDI will make the Soviet Union abandon its ICBM force, or that it will necessarily eliminate the Soviet preemptive option. The Soviet Union is likely to want to retain, and perhaps to expand, its offensive forces in order to ensure that they can penetrate or evade the defense.

Anti-Satellite Weapons

The second response the Soviet Union could make is to develop and deploy systems to attack and destroy key elements of a U.S. space-based BMD system. Space mines, anti-satellite weapons, and ground-based lasers, for example, could attack space-based components of the BMD system, while its ground-based elements could be threatened by cruise missiles or other off-shore systems.

The Soviet Union has developed a primitive ASAT weapon, and has been working on the use of lasers for ASAT purposes. According to the latest edition of the Defense Department's *Soviet Military Power*, the Soviet Union could construct "ground-based laser anti-satellite (ASAT) facilities at operational sites" by the end of the 1980s and "may deploy operational systems of space-based lasers for anti-satellite purposes in the 1990s, if their technology developments prove successful." Velikhov has pointed to the need for the Soviet Union to develop the capability to destroy a space-based BMD system. It is possible that R&D in this area has already been stepped up. The Soviet ASAT program did not have high priority in the 1970s, but it could now be given top priority as a possible counter to space-based BMD.[16]

The acquisition of weapons that could destroy the space-based BMD system would increase the Soviet Union's offensive options, and would fit in well with dominant features of Soviet strategic thought. This would require a significant R&D effort on the Soviet Union's part, but such an effort is well in hand. . . .

Ballistic Missile Defense

The third response the Soviet Union could make to the SDI is to deploy a BMD system of its own. It was argued above that the reasons why the Soviet Union limited its BMD deployment in the 1960s still seem to be valid. But this would change if the U.S. moved to deploy strategic defenses, because once the fears that now restrain Soviet BMD activities are realized, the motive for restraint would disappear. The only concern that would remain would be cost-effectiveness.

The Soviet Union might build a BMD system in order to enhance the survivability of its offensive missiles. So far, it has tried to cope with ICBM vulnerability by developing mobile ICBMs, by diversifying its strategic forces, and perhaps by adopting a launch-under-attack policy, but it might deploy BMD if the problem became serious enough. If the United States deploys BMD, the issue of vulnerability will become more important for the Soviet Union, because it will want to ensure that as large a proportion of its offensive forces as possible will be available for retaliation if the United States should strike first. BMD deployment by the United States would thus put pressure on the Soviet Union to deploy its own system.

Apart from such strategic considerations, there are political factors that will encourage the Soviet Union to deploy BMD if the United States does so. The SDI program calls for technology demonstrations before 1990, and these will be seen as symbols of American military and technological power. The Soviet Union may well feel impelled, as it has so often in the past, to try to match the United States program. The heavy stress that the Soviet leaders lay on parity in their strategic relationship with the United States will push them in this direction.

If the Soviet leaders become convinced that the United States is going to proceed to BMD deployment, they might decide to make a "preemptive breakout" from the ABM treaty by building their own conventional BMD system on a nationwide scale. They might do this to show that the Soviet Union would not be overtaken in a BMD race, to complicate United States military plans, or in the hope of gaining some advantage in arms-control negotiations. . . .

SOVIET-AMERICAN RELATIONS AND ARMS CONTROL

The Soviet Union can, in time, develop countermeasures to a possible space-based BMD system. But the Soviet leaders have also set themselves the more immediate goal of trying to stop or slow down the SDI through arms-control negotiations. They are evidently worried about the military and political aims of the United States, and fear that any superiority achieved through the deployment of BMD would not only give the United States a military advantage, but would also enable it to put political pressure on the Soviet Union. . . .

The Soviet leaders appear to be concerned also about the prospect of a costly technological race with the United States. Notwithstanding the advice of their scientific advisers, they may fear that the United States will develop a reasonably effective BMD system, and they will want, therefore, to forestall such a race. . . . In his speech to British members of Parliament in December 1984, Gorbachev said that the "non-militarization of space" and nuclear weapons "ought to be considered and resolved in [their] interconnection"—precisely the formulation that later appeared in the Shultz-Gromyko communiqué [of January 1985].[17]

The Soviet Union has insisted that successful reduction of offensive systems will be contingent on progress in limiting defensive systems. The Reagan administration, on the other hand, has reaffirmed its commitment to the SDI, and to the goal of moving towards a defense-dominant strategic relationship. . . . It is clear that the two sides have very different conceptions of the relationship between offensive and defensive systems, and this will make it difficult for them to reach agreement on arms control.

The SDI will also complicate negotiation of an ASAT agreement. The Soviet Union has pressed for such an agreement in recent years, within the broader framework of a treaty on the "militarization of space." Because ASAT systems would be one of the main Soviet responses to space-based BMD, the Soviet Union is not likely to conclude an ASAT agreement unless the United States abandons the goal of deploying space-based BMD. . . .

The Soviet Union has made it clear that it regards space weapons, and especially space-based BMD, as the most pressing issue for arms control. The United States, on the other hand, regards the reduction of offensive forces—especially the Soviet ICBM force—as a more urgent matter. Although the two sides have different goals, the possibility exists, in theory at any rate, of a trade-off between the Soviet interest in stopping the SDI and the United States interest in reducing offensive forces. A direct trade-off between the two areas is difficult to envisage, because the offensive systems are already operational, while space-based BMD is still at the research stage. Nevertheless, it is conceivable that agreements on offensive forces and defensive systems might be concluded which, although internally balanced, would be linked in the sense of being contingent on each other.

The obstacles in the way of such an agreement are considerable, however, because the two sides have different conceptions of the role of BMD in their strategic relationship. There are, besides, many difficult issues to be resolved in reaching agreement on intermediate-range and strategic nuclear forces. If the negotiations come to an impasse, the disagreements may become the focus of public accusations, of claims and counterclaims, by the two sides. The Soviet Union may make a concerted effort to encourage opposition to the SDI in the United States and Western Europe.

Unless remedial steps are taken—either unilaterally or through arms control—the net effect of the SDI on Soviet-American relations may well be to fuel the competition in offensive and defensive systems, thereby making the strategic relationship less stable; to complicate arms control, and perhaps to make it impossible; and to cast a shadow over political relations. The SDI will not provide escape from mutual deterrence, and may well make that relationship less stable and more fraught with suspicion and uncertainty.

In summary, the main appeal of the Strategic Defense Initiative is that it looks forward to a world in which the two superpowers would have defenses that would render nuclear weapons "impotent and obsolete." But as Richard DeLauer, former Under Secretary for Defense for Research and Engineering, has said, "with unconstrained proliferation [of offensive systems], no defensive system will work."[18] If defensive systems are to contribute to a safer and more stable strategic relationship between the United States and the Soviet Union, they will have to be embedded in a strict arms-control regime that limits offensive systems. In the current political and technological circumstances, however, the attempt to build defenses may well push the other side into expanding and upgrading its offensive forces. It is thus a paradox of the present superpower rivalry that the effort to build BMD can, and very possibly will, undermine the very condition that is needed to ensure that BMD contributes to a safer world.

NOTES

This article is an expanded and updated version of a discussion of the subject that appeared in *The Reagan Strategic Defense Initiative: A Technical, Political, and Arms Control Assessment*, a special report of the Center for International Security and Arms Control (Stanford: Stanford University, 1984). The author wishes to thank Sidney D. Drell, Philip J. Farley, Ted Postol, and George Smith for their help and advice.

1. V.D. Sokolovskii, *Voennaia strategiia* (Moscow: Voenizdat, 1962), p. 231.

2. *Krasnaia Zvezda*, Sept. 23, 1983.

3. Maj. Gen. V.M. Zemskov, "Wars of the Modern Era," *Voyennaya Mysl*, 1969, no. 5, FPD 0117/69, p. 60.

4. *Pravda*, Sept. 30, 1972.

5. *Krasnaia Zvezda*, Sept. 23, 1983. See also the article on military strategy in N.V. Ogarkov, ed., *Voennyi Entsiklopedicheskii Slovar'* (Moscow: Voenizdat, 1983), p. 712.

6. N.V. Ogarkov, *Vsegda v gotovnosti k zashchite otechestva* (Moscow: Voenizdat, 1982), p. 58.

7. See Clarence A. Robinson, Jr., "Soviets Accelerate Missile Defense Efforts," *Aviation Week & Space Technology*, Jan. 16, 1984, pp. 14-16.

8. On directed energy research, see Department of Defense, *Soviet Military Power*, 4th ed. (Washington, D.C.: U.S. Government Printing Office, 1985), pp. 43-5. See also the FY 1983 *Department of Defense Program for Research, Development and Acquisition*, statement by the Hon. Richard D. DeLauer, Under Secretary of Defense for Research and Engineering, to the 97th Congress (Washington, D.C.: U.S. Department of Defense, 1982), pp. 11-21.

9. *Pravda*, March 27, 1983.

10. *Pravda*, July 12 and Oct. 27, 1982.

11. *Pravda*, July 12, 1982.

12. Dr. George A. Keyworth, "The Case for Strategic Defense: An Option for a World Disarmed," in *Issues in Science and Technology*, Fall 1984, p. 42.

13. Central Intelligence Agency, *Estimated Soviet Defense Spending in Rubles, 1970–1975*, SR 76-10121U, May 1976; Central Intelligence Agency, *Estimated Soviet Defense Spending: Trends and Prospects*, SR 78-10121, June 1978.

14. Dr. George Keyworth, *Reassessing Strategic Defense* (Washington, D.C.: Council on Foreign Relations, Feb. 15, 1984), p. 18.

15. Keyworth, loc. cit., in *Issues in Science and Technology*, p. 38.

16. Department of Defense, *Soviet Military Power*, 4th ed. (Washington, D.C.: U.S. Government Printing Office, 1985), p. 44; interview with Velikhov on Radio Moscow, May 25, 1984, *Foreign Broadcast Information Service*, June 6, 1984, USSR International Affairs, p. AAII; on the Soviet ASAT program see Stephen M. Meyer, "Soviet Military Programmes and the 'New High Ground,'" *Survival*, Sept.-Oct. 1983, pp. 204-215.

17. *Pravda*, Dec. 19, 1984, p. 4.

18. Richard Halloran, "Higher Budget Foreseen for Advanced Missiles," *New York Times*, May 18, 1983, p. 11.

CHAPTER 15

Report to Congress After Geneva Summit

Ronald Reagan

Mr. Speaker, Mr. President, Members of the Congress, distinguished guests, my fellow Americans:

As you know, I have just come from Geneva and talks with General Secretary Gorbachev. In the past few days, we spent over 15 hours in various meetings with the General Secretary and the members of his official party. Approximately five of those hours were talks between Mr. Gorbachev and myself, one on one. That was the best part—our fireside summit.

There will be, I know, a great deal of commentary and opinion as to what the meetings produced and what they were like. There were over 3,000 reporters in Geneva, so it's possible there will be 3,000 opinions on what happened. Maybe it's the old broadcaster in me but I decided to file my own report directly to you.

'WE MADE THAT START'

We met, as we had to meet. I had called for a fresh start—and we made that start. I can't claim we had a meeting of the minds on such fundamentals as ideology or national purpose—but we understand each other better. That's the key to peace. I gained a better perspective; I feel he did, too.

It was a constructive meeting. So constructive, in fact, that I look forward to welcoming Mr. Gorbachev to the United States next year. And I have accepted his invitation to go to Moscow the following year.

I found Mr. Gorbachev to be an energetic defender of Soviet policy. He was an eloquent speaker, and a good listener. Our subject matter was shaped by the facts of this century.

These past 40 years have not been an easy time for the West or the world. You know the facts; there is no need to recite the historical record. Suffice it to say that the United States cannot afford illusions about the

Excerpted from the *New York Times*, "Text of Reagan Report to Congress," November 22, 1985, p. 8.

nature of the U.S.S.R. We cannot assume that their ideology and purpose will change. . . .

We discussed nuclear arms and how to reduce them. I explained our proposals for equitable, verifiable and deep reductions. I outlined my conviction that our proposals would make not just for a world that seemed safer but that really is safer.

I am pleased to report tonight that General Secretary Gorbachev and I did make a measure of progress here. While we still have a long ways to go, we're at least heading in the right direction. We moved arms control forward from where we were last January, when the Soviets returned to the table.

We are both instructing our negotiators to hasten their vital work. The world is waiting for results.

PLEDGE TO CUT NUCLEAR ARMS

Specifically, we agreed in Geneva that each side should move to cut offensive nuclear arms by 50 percent in appropriate categories. In our joint statement we called for early progress on this, turning the talks toward our chief goal, offensive reductions. We called for an interim accord on intermediate-range nuclear forces, leading, I hope, to the complete elimination of this class of missiles. All this with tough verification.

We also made progress in combating together the spread of nuclear weapons, an arms control area in which we've cooperated effectively over the years. We are also opening a dialogue on combating the spread and use of chemical weapons, while moving to ban them altogether. Other arms control dialogue—in Vienna on conventional forces, and in Stockholm on lessening the chances for a surprise attack in Europe—also received a boost. Finally, we agreed to begin work on risk reduction centers, a decision that should give special satisfaction to Senators Nunn and Warner, who so ably promoted this idea.

HE DESCRIBED HIS PLAN

I described our Strategic Defense Initiative—our research effort that envisions the possibility of defensive systems which could ultimately protect all nations against the danger of nuclear war. This discussion produced a very direct exchange of views.

Mr. Gorbachev insisted that we might use a strategic defense system to put offensive weapons into space and establish nuclear superiority.

I made it clear that S.D.I. has nothing to do with offensive weapons; that, instead, we are investigating non-nuclear defensive systems that would only threaten offensive missiles, not people. If our research succeeds, it will bring much closer the safer, more stable world we seek. Nations could defend themselves against missile attack, and mankind, at long last, escape the prison of mutual terror—this is my dream.

So I welcomed the chance to tell Mr. Gorbachev that we are a nation that defends, rather than attacks, that our alliances are defensive, not offensive. We don't seek nuclear superiority. We do not seek a first strike advantage over the Soviet Union. Indeed, one of my fundamental arms control objectives is to get rid of first-strike weapons altogether.

This is why we have proposed a 50 percent reduction in the most threatening nuclear weapons, especially those that could carry out a first strike.

I went further in expressing our peaceful intentions. I described our proposal in the Geneva negotiations for a reciprocal program of open laboratories and strategic defense research. We are offering to permit Soviet experts to see first hand that S.D.I. does not involve offensive weapons. American scientists would be allowed to visit comparable facilities of the Soviet strategic defensive program, which, in fact, has involved much more than research for many years.

WORLDWIDE MISSILE DEFENSE

Finally, I reassured Mr. Gorbachev on another point. I promised that if our research reveals that a defense against nuclear missiles is possible, we would sit down with our allies and the Soviet Union to see how together we could replace all strategic ballistic missiles with such a defense, which threatens no one. . . .

We remain far apart on a number of issues, as had to be expected. However, we reached agreement on a number of matters, and, as I mentioned, we agreed to continue meeting, and this is important and very good. There's always room for movement, action and progress when people are talking to each other instead of talking about each other.

NEW AGREEMENT ON CULTURE

We have concluded a new agreement designed to bring the best of America's artists and academics to the Soviet Union. The exhibits that will be included in this exchange are one of the most effective ways for the average Soviet citizen to learn about our way of life. This agreement will also expand the opportunities for Americans to experience the Soviet people's rich cultural heritage, because their artists and academics will be coming here.

We have also decided to go forward with a number of people-to-people initiatives that will go beyond greater contact not only between the political leaders of our two countries but our respective students, teachers, and others as well. We have emphasized youth exchanges. This will help break down stereotypes, build friendships, and, frankly, provide an alternative to propaganda.

We have agreed to establish a new Soviet consulate in New York and a new American consulate in Kiev. This will bring a permanent U.S. presence to the Ukraine for the first time in decades.

We have also, together with the Government of Japan, concluded a Pacific air safety agreement with the Soviet Union. This is designed to set up cooperative measures to improve civil air safety in that region. What happened before must never be allowed to happen again.

As a potential way of dealing with the energy needs of the world of the future, we have also advocated international cooperation to explore the feasibility of developing fusion energy.

All of these steps are part of a long-term effort to build a more stable relationship with the Soviet Union. No one ever said it would be easy. But we've come a long way. . . .

CHAPTER 16

The Nuclear and Space Arms Talks: Where We Are After the Summit

Paul H. Nitze

. . . The November summit and the autumn events leading up to it represent not only the possibility for a fresh start in the U.S.-Soviet relationship but mark what we hope is the beginning of a genuine process of give-and-take in the nuclear and space arms talks. The barriers to agreement are, however, substantial.

SOVIET COUNTERPROPOSAL

The first break in the ice came at the end of September with the tabling of a Soviet counterproposal to our March 1985 offer. While the effects of that counterproposal would be inequitable and destabilizing, it also contains, as the President expressed it, "seeds which should be nurtured."

The Soviet offer consists of various bans and freezes, as well as limits on and reductions in offensive forces.

• "Strategic delivery systems" would be reduced by 50%, to a level of 1,250 for the U.S.S.R. and 1,680 for the United States. However, the Soviet definition of strategic delivery vehicles would also cover, on the U.S. side, LRINF missiles and "medium-range" nuclear-capable aircraft in Europe, in Asia, and on all of our aircraft carriers, while about 2,000 comparable Soviet nuclear delivery vehicles, as well as 300 Backfire bombers, would not be limited. Thus, were the United States to retain equality in strategic nuclear delivery vehicles, it would have to cut LRINF missiles and dual-capable aircraft to 430, 20% of the current Soviet level. If the United States were to retain LRINF missiles and dual-capable aircraft at current levels, it would

Excerpted from U.S. Department of State, Current Policy No. 770, December 5, 1985.

have to cut strategic nuclear delivery vehicles to less than half the allowed Soviet number.

- "Nuclear charges" would be sharply reduced to a level of 6,000. However, they would be defined to include the gravity bombs and short-range attack missiles carried by U.S. heavy and medium-range bombers. By counting such bomber weapons as equivalent to Soviet ballistic missile RVs, despite the massive Soviet air defenses faced by bombers and the lower readiness rate of bombers compared to ballistic missiles, the United States would be significantly penalized.
- "Charges" on any one component (that is, ICBMs, SLBMs, or bombers) would be reduced to 60% of the total, leading to a maximum level of 3,600 ICBM RVs. Although this sublimit would represent a major reduction, Soviet prompt counterforce capabilities would actually grow against the reduced number of U.S. hardened facilities.
- All cruise missiles with ranges above 600 kilometers would be banned, terminating the U.S. ALCM, SLCM, and GLCM programs.
- All "new" nuclear delivery systems would be banned, probably precluding the U.S. D-5 and Midgetman missiles and advanced technology bomber, while allowing the Soviet SS-25, SS-X-24 and SS-NX-23 missiles and Blackjack heavy bomber.
- Research, development, and deployment of "space-strike arms" would be banned, halting the U.S. SDI program and allowing many Soviet ABM activities to continue.

In sum, despite significant reductions, the Soviet counterproposal would block U.S. strategic defense programs while allowing Soviet programs to proceed; it would halt the modernization of U.S. strategic offensive forces; and it would include in reductions U.S. systems which defend our allies and exclude Soviet systems which threaten them. The net effect would be a lopsided nuclear balance, a weakened U.S. deterrent, and decreased stability for both sides.

However, in spite of its numerous flaws, the detailed Soviet counterproposal did include the principle of deep cuts in strategic offensive arms and, along with subsequent offers in Geneva, seemed to contemplate an interim INF outcome which would allow for U.S. LRINF missiles in Europe. Building on such positive elements, President Reagan directed that a new U.S. proposal be advanced at the negotiations on November 1.

U.S. NOVEMBER PROPOSAL

Strategic Offensive Arms. The new U.S. proposal builds on the 50% reduction concept in a constructive and equitable way.

- Reentry vehicles on ICBMs and SLBMs would be reduced to a limit of 4,500—about 50% below current levels.
- Reentry vehicles on ICBMs would be reduced to 3,000—about 50% below the current Soviet level and roughly halfway between our earlier proposal for a limit of 2,500 and their proposed limit of 3,600.

• The highest overall strategic ballistic missile throw-weight of either side would be reduced by 50%, in this case, from the Soviet level of 11.9 million pounds. (By way of comparison, the United States has 4.4 million pounds.)

• Contingent upon acceptance of RV and throw-weight limits, the United States would accept equal limits of 1,500 on the number of long-range ALCMs carried by U.S. and Soviet heavy bombers—about 50% below planned U.S. deployment levels.

• For reasons previously alluded to, the United States cannot agree to one common limit on ballistic missile RVs and ALCMs. But if the Soviets were to accept our proposed limit of 4,500 RVs along with our proposed limit of 1,500 ALCMs, it would result in reduction to a total of 6,000 ballistic missile RVs and ALCMs on each side.

With respect to strategic nuclear delivery vehicles, the United States has proposed a reduction in strategic ballistic missiles to a limit of 1,250–1,450, or about 40–45% below the current higher Soviet level. In this context, the United States could accept further reduction of heavy bomber limits to 350 (compared to our earlier proposal of 400)—about 40% below the current U.S. SALT-accountable level.

For reasons similar to those applying to an RV and ALCM aggregate, the United States cannot agree to the Soviet proposal to include in a single aggregate strategic ballistic missiles and heavy bombers. However, if agreement were reached on a range of 1,250–1,450 for ICBMs and SLBMs, and on heavy bomber limits of 350, it would result in reduction of the total of strategic ballistic missiles and heavy bombers to between 1,600 and 1,800.

The U.S. proposal also contains a ban on the development and deployment of all new heavy strategic ballistic missiles and on the modernization of existing heavy missiles due to the destabilizing character of such systems. All mobile ICBMs would also be banned because of inherent verification difficulties and asymmetries in deployment opportunities between the sides. "Builddown" is the suggested means of implementing the agreed reductions.

Intermediate-Range Nuclear Forces. With respect to intermediate-range nuclear forces, the United States continues to prefer total elimination of the entire class of U.S. and Soviet LRINF missiles. Thus, our previous proposals remain on the table. We have also made a new proposal as an interim step toward this goal.

• The United States would cap its own LRINF missile launcher deployments in Europe at the number deployed as of December 31, 1985 (140 Pershing II and GLCM) in return for Soviet agreement to reduce SS-20 missile launchers within range of NATO Europe to the same number.

• There would be freedom to mix between systems deployed as of December 31, 1985, but the mix would be a subject for discussion. For example, we could agree on a mix giving the United States an approximately equal number at around 420 to 450 LRINF missile warheads in NATO Europe (based on 4 warheads per GLCM launcher, 1 warhead per Pershing II launcher, and 3 warheads per SS-20 launcher).

• The Soviets would be required to reduce SS-20 launchers in Asia (not within range of NATO Europe) by the same proportion as the reduction

of launchers within range of NATO Europe. The end result would be equal global LRINF warhead limits.
 • Appropriate constraints would also be applied to shorter range INF missiles.

Defense and Space. With respect to defense and space, the United States has made clear that we are committed to the SDI research program, which is being carried out in compliance with the ABM Treaty. We seek a Soviet commitment to explore with us now how a cooperative transition could be accomplished, should new defensive technologies prove feasible. We are also proposing that the Soviets join us, even now, in an "open laboratories" arrangement under which both sides would provide information on each other's strategic defense research programs and provide reciprocal opportunities for visiting associated research facilities and laboratories.

Verification and Compliance. The United States continues to stress the critical importance of agreeing to effective means of verification so as to be able to assess with confidence compliance with provisions of all agreements resulting from the negotiations. The importance of verification is more evident now then it was before, given Soviet violations of existing arms control agreements.

The United States continues to stress the need for the Soviets to take necessary steps to correct current instances of noncompliance with existing arms control agreements, for noncompliance is both politically corrosive and militarily hazardous. Restoring compliance is, thus, a critical step.

The Soviet Union must alter current practices which obstruct U.S. verification of compliance. One initial step is for Soviets to alter their current encryption of telemetry and revert to telemetry practices in use at the time of signing of SALT II. This is militarily important in its own right and is also of considerable political significance.

THE NOVEMBER SUMMIT

You know the duration of the sessions at the November summit between President Reagan and General Secretary Gorbachev: some 5 hours of one-on-one dialogue and more than 8 hours of discussion in plenary. The two leaders had an intensive and frank examination of the issues in all four agenda categories. The potential intangible benefits to be derived from the development of personal rapport between these two men is obvious, so I will confine my observations to the language relating to the nuclear and space talks which appeared in the joint statement published at the conclusion of the summit and to a discussion of issues it addresses.

We were able in the joint statement to achieve Soviet commitment to early progress in the negotiations, focusing particularly on "the principle of 50% reductions in the nuclear arms of the U.S. and USSR appropriately applied" and "the idea of an interim INF agreement." As I have already mentioned, these concepts are common elements in the fall proposals of the two sides, but it is not clear that the Soviets do not still link such language to termination of the U.S. Strategic Defense Initiative. SDI is, of course, not mentioned at all in the joint statement. The Soviets were content, in the end, to repeat the language of the joint agreement of January 8, 1985, which included the goal of preventing an arms race in space. We have made abundantly clear to the Soviets that, in our view, SDI is consistent with this goal; we are calling for a cooperative approach to the deployment of defensive systems—as opposed to a "race"—were our research, or theirs, to demonstrate that such systems could help the world get rid of the threat of mutual destruction.

I would highlight another passage in the joint statement: "During the negotiation of these agreements, effective measures for verification of compliance with obligations assumed will be agreed upon." It will be useful for us during the negotiations to have this acknowledgment that effective verification measures must be devised concurrently with the resolution of other issues. It represents another modest step in our efforts to put verification concerns on a par with the reductions or limitations themselves.

One of the less encouraging aspects of the summit was Gorbachev's unwavering opposition to SDI. There were, indeed, no signs of movement from even the most untenable elements of the Soviet position on strategic defenses, such as the proposed ban on all research. The Soviets also refused to move from any of their fundamentally unacceptable positions on START and on INF. More encouraging are the growing indications that the Soviets may be willing seriously to discuss all three aspects of the negotiatioins concurrently when the nuclear and space arms talks resume in Geneva in January without demanding a prior agreement on a ban on SDI research.

It is also noteworthy that the President seems to have made some progress in convincing Gorbachev that he is sincere in his stated intentions for SDI, even though the Soviet leader vigorously disputed the President's conclusions about its consequences.

During the next round of the nuclear and space arms talks, commencing on January 16, 1986, we will be able to judge the Soviet implementation of our mutual commitment to accelerate work. We plan to spend the opening weeks describing our November 1 proposal in greater detail. Max Kampelman,[1] Senator Tower,[2] and Mike Glitman[3] will have authority to explore opportunities for give-and-take. We hope to elicit constructive responses from the Soviet side so that we may then be able to report that they are engaged in a genuine process of serious negotiation toward balanced and verifiable agreements which will improve stability and reduce the risk of war.

NOTES

1. Max M. Kampelman, Head of U.S. Delegation on Arms Control Negotiations and U.S. Negotiator on Defense and Space Arms.

2. John Tower, U.S. Negotiator on Strategic Nuclear Arms.

3. Maynard W. Glitman, U.S. Negotiator on Intermediate-Range Nuclear Arms.

Bibliography: Part Four

Arbatov, G. "Arbatov Assails Star Wars Research." *Pravda,* July 1, 1985, p. 6, in *Current Digest of the Soviet Press,* July 24, 1985, p. 7.

Dean, Jonathan. "Will NATO Survive Ballistic Missile Defense?" *Journal of International Affairs* (Summer 1985):95–114.

Garthoff, Raymond L. "BMD and East-West Relations." In Ashton B. Carter and David N. Schwartz, eds., *Ballistic Missile Defense.* Washington, D.C.: Brookings, 1984.

Gorbachev, Mikhail S. "Excerpts from Gorbachev News Session: 'All Have a Stake.'" *New York Times,* November 22, 1985.

Jasani, Bhupendra, ed. *Space Weapons—The Arms Control Dilemma.* Philadelphia: Taylor and Francis, 1985.

Kupperman, Robert H. "Using SDI to Reshape Soviet Strategic Behavior." *Washington Quarterly* (Summer 1985):77–84.

Meyer, Stephen M. "Soviet Strategic Programmes and the U.S. SDI." *Survival* (November/December 1985):274–292.

Nitze, Paul H. "SDI: Its Nature and Rationale," address before the North Atlantic Assembly, San Francisco, California, October 15, 1985. Reprinted in U.S. State Department, Bureau of Public Affairs, Current Policy No. 751, October 1985, pp. 1–3.

Payne, Keith B., and Colin S. Gray. "Nuclear Policy and the Defensive Transition." *Foreign Affairs* (Spring 1984):820–842.

Sagdayev, Roald, and Andrei Kokoshin, study directors. "Space-Based Defences: A Soviet Study." *Survival* (March/April 1985):83–89.

Yost, David S. "Soviet Ballistic Missile Defense and NATO." *Orbis* (Summer 1985):281–292.

PART FIVE

SDI AND U.S.-ALLIED RELATIONS

The initial reaction of the West European allies to SDI was almost unanimously negative. They doubted its technical and strategic feasibility, feared its effect on the unity of the alliance, and worried about the negative impact on U.S.-Soviet relations and the prospects of arms control.

The ferocity of their initial opposition to SDI is revealed in Christoph Bertram's article. Bertram, former director of the influential International Institute for Strategic Studies in London, objected to SDI primarily because it seemed to be based on a fundamental misunderstanding of nuclear strategy and deterrence. In Bertram's view, which is shared by Sir Geoffrey Howe, Britain's foreign minister, deterrence cannot be altered or overcome by a technical innovation such as SDI. Worse, to try will drive the allies away from the United States, especially if SDI appears to protect the United States but not the European allies. Although the Reagan administration hurried to extend SDI's protection to Europe and offered to pursue defense against tactical as well as strategic missiles, European strategists were not reassured.

By 1986 a marked change had occurred in the public positions of the European governments. Britain and Germany signed agreements to engage in joint research on SDI with the United States. As their selections reveal, both Chancellor Helmut Kohl of West Germany and Prime Minister Margaret Thatcher of Great Britain spoke in favor of pursuing SDI, with the understanding that they would be consulted before deployment and that deployment itself would be subject to negotiations with the Soviet Union.

The European allies of the United States appear to have given their qualified support to SDI for several reasons. Perhaps the most important is their conclusion that the Reagan administration was serious about continuing the research and was willing, at least for the time being, to work within the limits of the ABM Treaty. A less important concern was the wish to share in the industrial research and development phases of SDI so as to avoid losing ground in the development of new technologies. Finally, it became clear that the potential damage to deterrence, arms control, and East-West relations could be minimized more effectively if the allied governments acted as partners rather than disaffected critics of the United States. The strategic value of SDI has yet to be agreed upon by the European allies and the Reagan administration.

CHAPTER 17

Strategic Defense and the Western Alliance

Christoph Bertram

The central issue in the American debate over the Strategic Defense Initiative understandably revolves around the extent to which strategic defenses could improve the security of the continental United States. Yet since the end of World War II, that security has been sustained in a collective system that links America to its allies in Europe and the Far East. The linchpin of these security alliances, which have been so successful in assuring postwar stability, has been the ability of U.S. strategic nuclear forces to deter a possible Soviet attack. . . .

Until now, the United States has maintained the credibility of that deterrent threat. The Strategic Defense Initiative, however, could fundamentally alter this state of affairs. With its promise to achieve an effective defense against nuclear weapons, and to alter the strategic relationship between the superpowers, the SDI concerns not only the U.S., but the security of its allies as well.

The European perspective on the SDI in particular, and weapons in space generally, is shaped by a number of factors. First, while European countries are becoming more active in space technology through their expanding civilian space programs, they are still bystanders rather than participants in the military uses of space. This will probably change over time; there are currently plans to develop European reconnaissance satellites and, at a much later date, a manned space station. Nonetheless, it will be many years before the Europeans even begin to approach the scale of military space operations that characterizes the U.S. and USSR programs.

Second, most Europeans have little more than instinctive reactions to proposals such as the Strategic Defense Initiative. The relative dependence of the Europeans on the U.S. for both information and concepts concerning new space-related technologies has hindered Europe from responding to the challenges that the SDI poses for strategic doctrine.

Excerpted by permission of the author and *Daedalus*, Journal of the American Academy of Arts and Sciences, Weapons in Space, Vol. II: Implications for Security, Summer 1985, Cambridge, Massachusetts.

Third, Europeans tend to view major technological developments in political, rather than military or even strategic terms. Their experience over the centuries has led them to conclude that security is, above all, a political task. Europeans ask, more persistently than Americans, what the political consequences of a new weapon system are likely to be. They suspect that, whatever new sophisticated weapons are being introduced, the political problems will remain the same. Many Europeans instinctively regard the introduction of major new military technologies either as a threat to stability or as a futile attempt to provide hardware answers to political questions.

My own view is that the space dimension of military competition will matter profoundly to Europe, just as it will to the superpowers. Regardless of whether the promises of the advocates are fulfilled, whether adequate defense against ballistic missiles is feasible, or whether the Soviet Union can keep pace with the United States in the arms race, the effect of a major, purposeful effort to deploy defensive weapons in space will be to generate a political shift of historic proportions. It will introduce into a remarkably stable strategic relationship between East and West an unprecedented degree of uncertainty and nervousness. And it will introduce into the European-American relationship—a relationship that despite repeated strains and occasional dissent has on balance remained harmonious and well-functioning—a profound rift that could break up the Western Alliance for good. . . .

BASIC ATTITUDES

In general, the European outlook on deterrence and the likely consequences of deploying weapons in space differs from the U.S. perspective in three important ways: Europeans, despite cyclical doubts, remain convinced that nuclear deterrence is essential to their security and that it can be based only on mutual assured destruction; they have a vested interest, both for international and domestic reasons, in East-West detente and arms control; and they are pursuing, through both the indigenous nuclear forces of France and Britain and the increasing European investment in the scientific and commercial aspects of space activities, interests of their own that are not always congruent with American interests.

Deterrence through Mutual Assured Destruction

Even though France and Britain have minimal nuclear forces, West Europeans fully recognize that their security depends on the nuclear guarantee of the United States and on the ability of either of the two superpowers to obliterate the other should deterrence fail. The potential for mutual assured destruction has seemed to most Europeans, with the exception of those totally opposed to all nuclear weapons, a logical and basically desirable condition. In the European historical experience, vulnerability is a natural state of affairs. With the exception of Great Britain, all European countries have in recent times experienced invasion, occupation, defeat, and victory. Deterrence based on mutual vulnerability corresponds to this experience.

Moreover, Europeans are profoundly convinced that their security rests on America's recognition of its *own* vulnerability. For Europeans, American-European solidarity is not just a matter of declared interests, but of shared fate. Herein lies the reason for the many logical contradictions evident in European arguments that in the past have often annoyed policy-makers and irritated public opinion in the United States. It also helps explain the European reluctance to rely primarily on conventional forces for their security, although this could reduce the likelihood that nuclear weapons might have to be used, as well as European opposition to such American nuclear weapons doctrines as the 1960s strategy calling for the early and massive use of tactical nuclear forces, or to the 1980s doctrine calling for selective nuclear operations, and thus to the militarily more relevant use of nuclear weapons. Finally, there is the European insistence that NATO policy not be predicated on the notion that a nuclear war could be limited to Europe.

These contradictions stem from the simple geographic fact of Western Europe's proximity to Soviet military power. West Europeans are convinced that the United States will remain vitally concerned about Europe only if its own survival is at stake. And they have no doubt that a nuclear war, however limited it may be, could well mean the end of the European states and European civilization.

This European attitude should not be dismissed merely as a parochial, regional perspective. In addition to the aim of tying the power of the United States to the fate of Europe, it reflects a more general view of the nature of strategic stability and security in the nuclear age. Its basic tenet is that war as a rational strategy has been overtaken by the dreadfulness of nuclear destruction. Accordingly, security cannot be based on the hope of either winning a nuclear war or successfully resisting a nuclear attack. Europeans are profoundly skeptical that any technological breakthrough will change this basic state of affairs; they instinctively adhere to the view that new military technologies will sooner or later be matched or countered by the other superpower. As a result, most Europeans tend to dismiss as apolitical those strategic abstractions frequently made by American thinkers concerning "intrawar deterrence," "escalation dominance," and "war-winning" or "prevailing" strategies. Even the important distinction between stabilizing and destabilizing technologies is met with skepticism. Most Europeans regard any major change in the structure of nuclear forces as either destabilizing, irrelevant, or both. They dismiss as inherently implausible the vision that new efforts in space might rid the world of the threat of nuclear devastation.

Detente and Arms Control

Americans may differ among themselves and with their European allies about the significance, prospects, and limitations of East-West cooperation. What distinguishes the European from the American debate, however, is that Europe, because of its geographical position, has no alternative to the persistent search for cooperation between East and West. America does have an alternative, one that has been reflected throughout its history in the tension between the isolationist and internationalist strains in American policy.

While Europeans do differ among themselves in the value they place on East-West relations, the experience of the past two decades has produced a consensus that transcends both regional and political differences. Nothing illuminates this more than the current political constellation in Western Europe. In France, there is a socialist government that, in contrast to its conservative predecessor, started off with deep misgivings about Soviet policies but has recently sought to intensify diplomatic contacts with Moscow. In Great Britain, the conservative government of Margaret Thatcher, outspoken in its Atlanticism and in its distrust of Soviet objectives, nonetheless emphasizes the need for constructive East-West relations. West Germany's liberal conservative government today pursues, virtually unchanged, that same *Ostpolitik* of its liberal Social Democratic predecessor it had once severely criticized. . . .

Specific European Interests in Space

. . . At present, both Britain and France are trying to keep abreast of the technological advances in the arsenals of the superpowers. France has decided on a major program to multiply the number of missile-carried warheads from the current 98 to 594 by the early 1990s, in particular through the introduction of MIRV technology, and little opposition has been voiced against these plans by any of the French political parties. In Great Britain, the Thatcher government has firmly committed itself to the purchase of Trident D-5 SLBMs from the United States. When deployed in the 1990s, the number of British warheads could increase from the current 64 to as many as 896 (assuming a maximum deployment of 14 warheads per missile). Although the opposition Labour Party is committed to canceling the program if the party should come to power, it is worth remembering that Labour has usually supported the British nuclear forces when in government. If anything curtails the size of the Trident program, it is more likely to be cost considerations than political opposition.

Even with the realization of these modernization programs, however, a major BMD effort by the Soviet Union would weaken French and British nuclear deterrence significantly. While most experts doubt that any BMD system could protect vital targets against a massive attack, such a large-scale attack would stretch the strategic capacity that France or Great Britain could mount, even with the expanded arsenals they are planning for the 1990s. . . .

EUROPEAN REACTIONS TO AMERICAN PROGRAMS: ABM AND SDI

. . . The Reagan administration has repeatedly emphasized that it seeks not merely to improve the current system of deterrence, but to effect a total reversal of strategy: from the predominance of deterrence by threat of second-strike retaliation, to the predominance of defense by threat of destroying attacking ballistic missiles in flight. It is this radical change in attitude—regardless of whether the strategic defenses are ever deployed—that is creating the deepest worry among the European governments.

These European concerns can be summarized as follows. First, it will be technically impossible to create a leak-proof defense against attacking missiles. An imperfect defense, on the other hand, will produce strategic instability, especially if both sides retain or increase their sizable offensive forces so as to overcome any projected defensive system. Moreover, the deployment of even an imperfect system could be interpreted by the adversary as an attempt to obtain a first-strike capability.

Second, Europeans suspect that the deployment of defenses will provide little additional security for Western Europe, bordering as it does on the countries of the Warsaw Pact. The result, they fear, will be a strategic decoupling of America's security from that of Western Europe, resulting in a "fortress America," with an unprotected and unprotectable *glacis* in Europe.[1]

Third, the bitter and protracted debate that took place in the early 1980s over the deployment of U.S. intermediate-range nuclear forces (INF) in Europe has left its mark. Those who favor the INF deployment believe that these systems foster an increased solidarity of risk within the Alliance, precisely because these weapons can reach targets in the Soviet Union, thus further exposing the U.S. to Soviet retaliation. Those who oppose INF, however, maintain that these systems manifest an American desire to limit a possible nuclear war to Europe. A major effort to build a BMD shield around the United States would undercut the arguments of those who have stood by the INF deployment decision.

Finally, Europeans are concerned with the impact of SDI on the resources of the Alliance as a whole. The SDI raises the specter of a new strategic arms race that could siphon off much-needed defense funds as well as scientific and industrial resources. Defense resources are likely to remain limited; even the United States will be unable to maintain its current defense spending increases in the face of mounting budget deficits. Given the enthusiasm in the White House for the SDI, Europeans fear that when the squeeze comes, the administration will not only increase pressure on them to carry more of the conventional military burden, but might also reduce its NATO related defense spending. An American preoccupation with strategic defense could thus weaken the existing defense in Europe.[2]

The Reagan administration has sought to diminish such fears by claiming that defense against missiles targeted on Western Europe is both possible and intended. But so far, European governments, including both political elites and most defense experts, have remained unpersuaded. Europeans, in short, doubt not only that BMD can improve NATO security; they profoundly question the wisdom of a shift from a policy of deterrence to a defense that most probably will remain very imperfect. Apart from a few isolated voices in European strategic circles, the European reaction to date has been almost unanimously hostile. . . .

Thus, President Reagan's vision of a world in which ballistic missiles have lost their threat is not shared by his European allies, even those who, by and large, stand firmly behind the stationing of American Pershing and cruise missiles in Europe. For, underlying the European misgivings is a deep fear that, once firmly underway, the SDI could shake the very foundation on which the Alliance and Western security have rested so far in the nuclear age.

SDI AND THE ESSENTIALS OF THE WESTERN ALLIANCE

. . . From the European perspective, the major issue is whether only U.S. targets would be protected against ballistic missile attacks, or those in Western Europe as well. If the former were true, then clearly the sense of shared risks between Europe and the United States would be called into question. Extended deterrence would cease to be credible, and the only credible use of Soviet nuclear forces would be against non-American allied targets (i.e., in Western Europe and the Far East). Similarly, the only credible use of U.S. nuclear forces would be against targets outside the USSR (i.e., in Eastern Europe). In short, this would conjure up the vision of a nuclear war limited to Europe, a scenario the West Europeans have been striving for thirty years to avoid.

The consequences of this would be politically unbearable for the Western Alliance. America's European allies would lose what they have always regarded as an essential component of their security: the deterrent effect of the link to the U.S. strategic nuclear arsenal. Neither American nuclear forces stationed in Europe nor indigenous European strategic forces could make up for this loss of security. Because it would be possible for the first time in the nuclear age to limit nuclear conflict to the European region, the deterrent effect of American tactical nuclear forces (TNF) in Europe would be reduced to the damage their limited use could inflict. No longer would this be backed by the uncertainty of escalation. A preemptive Soviet strike against American tactical nuclear forces in Europe would lose its risk for the attacker, just as a nuclear strike against other Western European targets would, for the first time, become militarily rational. An increased effort to build up indigenous nuclear forces in Europe would merely multiply systems that have lost their threat. Europeans would simply be relying on deterrent forces that could be blunted by Soviet action but that could not retaliate against Soviet territory. Even if the Western Europeans should try to circumvent Soviet defenses against ballistic weapons by opting for nonballistic nuclear delivery vehicles instead, the absence of the threat of American nuclear involvement would deprive such a move of any significant deterrent effect.

In other words, Western Europe would find itself for the first time in the history of the Atlantic Alliance exposed to the very strategic situation the Alliance was created to avoid: a Soviet superiority in nuclear and conventional military strength that could not be offset by the threat of U.S. strategic involvement in a European war.

Would European reaction to the Reagan proposals change significantly if the defensive shield against ballistic missile attack were to cover *both* the United States and its European allies (assuming, on the other side, that the Soviet Union would extend its defensive shield over its East European allies)? Probably not, although Western European governments in their first reactions to the Strategic Defense Initiative have implied otherwise. Leaving aside the political problem of the presence of additional large-scale missile deployments in Europe, the major feature of a BMD world would remain: the security cord of potential escalation to the strategic nuclear level between Europe and the United States would be broken. The risk for the Soviet Union of a major attack against Western Europe would be significantly lower than it has been throughout the nuclear age. Moreover, even if a BMD shield were to cover Europe as well, the Allies would, by the mere fact of geography, remain exposed to other nuclear weapon attacks: by artillery, aircraft, or cruise missiles.

Conversely, the other side of the Atlantic would remain relatively protected by sheer geography against shorter-range or slow-flying nonballistic nuclear systems. At the same time, the U.S. would be unable to deter Soviet action by raising the specter that any major conflict might escalate to the nuclear strategic level.

But could not *some* degree of defense against missile attacks—the protection of vulnerable military targets such as missile silos and command centers, for example—enhance the deterrent capability of the Alliance? Could not a certain measure of protection for strategic forces and command centers enhance strategic stability by improving the survivability of second-strike forces, thus gaining time for controlled reaction in case of crisis and war?

If this were a realistic objective, it might be possible to reconcile American and European views. However, the SDI philosophy of the Reagan administration is quite opposed to any limitation of defensive capabilities to specific military targets. Whatever limited protection might become possible is not an end in itself, but a step towards the ultimate objective: to replace deterrence by defense. As long as this is the case, it matters little for America's allies (or, indeed, her opponents) whether the outcome will remain modest in the end. What matters is the strategic conviction behind it. The vision of a leakproof defensive system that would remove the threat of nuclear missiles is a political objective, an expression of what the administration would like to achieve and an indication of its view of a desirable strategic future. This view is incompatible with the European understanding of, and European interests in, the Western Alliance. . . .

The SDI therefore risks undermining, on the U.S. side, the basic bargain of the Alliance, and on the European side, the acceptability of nuclear weapons and nuclear deterrence. Furthermore, the two trends are reinforcing each other. The more Europeans display an aversion to nuclear weapons, the more the United States will avoid committing its security to the uncertainties of European politics.

The final question is this: is it worth risking the future of the Western Alliance for the sake of uncertain and doubtful technological promises? Is it worth, on such shaky foundations, instilling in Europeans the fear that they will be left to themselves in the face of Soviet military power, and in Americans the illusion that a European war would not profoundly shake their own security? Since the birth of the Alliance, the Soviet Union has understandably sought to undermine the unity of the West. So far, it has not succeeded; Western cohesion has remained strong.

Ironically, those who believe that the world can be made safe against nuclear attack will themselves end up undermining this cohesion.

NOTES

1. These doubts were first formulated by West German Defense Minister Manfred Wörner, with the apparent approval of his European colleagues, after they were briefed on the SDI by Caspar Weinberger at a meeting of NATO's Nuclear Planning Group, held in Turkey in April 1984. See *Süddeutsche Zeitung*, April 5, 1984.

2. This also seems to be the reason why U.S. General Bernard Rogers, the Supreme Allied Commander in Europe, has repeatedly displayed skepticism towards the SDI project.

CHAPTER 18

Defence and Security in the Nuclear Age

Sir Geoffrey Howe

Much has been said and written about President Reagan's Strategic Defence Initiative. The first point to make is that, as US spokesmen have made clear, this is a research programme, conducted in full conformity with the limits of the ABM Treaty. As a research programme, it is also full of questions. The answers may be clear or obscure. They may not even emerge at all. As the US administration themselves recognize, the programme is geared to a concept, which may in the end prove elusive.

The second point is that treaty obligations specifically allow for research to continue into defensive systems. Evidently, it is pointless to try to impose constraints which cannot be verified. Most activities in laboratories or research institutes come into that category. The ABM Treaty recognised this when it drew a distinction between research on the one hand and development, testing and deployment on the other.

The third, equally important point is that a balance must always be maintained between US and Soviet capabilities, in research as in other aspects. Given what we know of Soviet activities in the research field over a number of years, there is a clear need for the United States to match the present stage in Soviet programmes. It is for this reason that the Prime Minister has repeatedly expressed our firm conviction that US research should go ahead.

But what should happen if and when decisions are required on moving from the research to the development stage?

In evaluating the results of research, and in taking any such decisions, we shall need to ask ourselves some very basic questions about the future nature of Western strategy. In particular, we shall have to consider how best to enhance deterrence, how best to curb rather than stimulate a new arms race. At that stage, the judgements to be made will only partly depend upon technical assessments about the feasibility of defences. Even if the

Excerpted from the text of an address at the Royal United Services Institute, London, March 15, 1985.

research shows promise, the case for proceeding will have to be weighed in the light of the wider strategic implications of moving down the defensive road.

But can we afford even now simply to wait for the scientists and military experts to deliver their results at some later stage? Have we a breathing space of five, ten, fifteen years before we need to address strategic concerns? I do not believe so. The history of weapons development and the strategic balance shows only too clearly that research into new weapons and study of their strategic implications must go hand in hand. Otherwise, research may acquire an unstoppable momentum of its own, even though the case for stopping may strengthen with the passage of years. Prevention may be better than later attempts at a cure. We must take care that political decisions are not pre-empted by the march of technology, still less by premature attempts to predict the route of that march.

The questions to be faced are complex and difficult.

There would inevitably be risks in a radical alteration of the present basis for Western security. How far would these risks be offset by the attractions of adopting a more defensive posture: That is to say, of developing what might prove to be only a limited defence against weapons of devastating destructive force. Could the process of moving towards a greater emphasis on active defences be managed without generating dangerous uncertainty?

Let us assume that limited defences began to prove possible, and key installations began to be protected by active defences. In his 1983 address President Reagan himself acknowledged that a mix of offensive and defensive systems could be "viewed as fostering an aggressive policy." Uncertainty apart, would the establishment of limited defences increase the threat to civilian populations by stimulating a return to the targeting policies of the 1950s?

Most fundamental of all, would the supposed technology actually work? And would it, as Mr. Paul Nitze has noted, provide defences that not only worked but were survivable and cost-effective? These are the key questions to be answered by the research that is being undertaken on both sides.

It would be wrong to underestimate the enormous technological expertise and potential of the United States. But, as we all recognise, there would be no advantage in creating a new Maginot Line of the twenty-first century, liable to be outflanked by relatively simpler and demonstrably cheaper counter-measures. If the technology does work, what will be its psychological impact on the other side? President Reagan has repeatedly made it clear that he does not seek superiority. But we would have to ensure that the perceptions of others were not different.

What are the chances that there would be no outright winner in the everlasting marathon of the arms race? And if the ballistic missile indeed showed signs of becoming, in President Reagan's words, impotent and obsolete, how would protection be extended against the non-ballistic nuclear threat, the threat posed by aircraft or cruise missiles, battlefield nuclear weapons or, in the last resort, by covert action? What other defences in addition to space-based systems would need to be developed, and at what cost, to meet these continuing threats?

If it initially proved feasible to construct only limited defences, these would be bound to be more vulnerable than comprehensive systems to counter-measures. Would these holes in the dyke produce and even encourage a nuclear flood? Leaving aside the threat to civilian populations, would active defences provide the only feasible way of protecting key military installations? Might we be better advised to employ other methods of protection, such as more mobile and under-sea forces?

Finally on the technology side, could we be certain that the new systems would permit adequate political control over both nuclear weapons and defensive systems, or might we find ourselves in a situation where the peace of the world rested solely upon computers and automatic decision-making?

Then there is the question of cost. The financial burden of developing and deploying defences goes far beyond the additional cost of providing defences against the non-ballistic missile threat. No-one at present can provide even a guestimate of the total sums involved. But it is fair to assume that these will run into many hundreds of billions of dollars.

We know only too well that our defences must be cut to the cloth of our financial resources. We shall have to ask ourselves not only whether the West can afford active defences against nuclear missiles. We must also ask whether the enormous funds to be devoted to such systems might be better employed.

Are there more cost-effective and affordable ways of enhancing deterrence? Might it be better to use the available funds to improve our capability to oppose a potential aggressor at a time of crisis with a credible, sustainable and controllable mix of conventional and nuclear forces? In short, how far will we be able to impose new burdens on defence budgets already under strain? And what would be the effect on all the other elements of our defences, on which Western security will continue in large part to depend?

The implications for arms control must also be carefully considered. Would the prospect of new defences being deployed inexorably crank up the levels of offensive nuclear systems designed to overwhelm them? History and the present state of technology suggest that this risk cannot be ignored. Or could the same prospect—the vision of effective defences over the horizon—provide new incentives to both sides to start at once on reducing their present levels? This explains the importance of the second point agreed at Camp David last December.

In his statement to Congress last month President Reagan spoke of the need to reverse the erosion of the ABM Treaty. It represents a political and military keystone in the still shaky arch of security we have constructed with the East over the past decade and a half. But to go beyond research into defensive systems would be inconsistent with the terms of the ABM Treaty as it stands. It was agreed at Camp David last December that any deployment beyond those limits would have to be a matter for negotiation. We would have to be confident that that formidable task could actually be managed on a mutually acceptable basis.

We have heard recently from Moscow a lot of dogmatic statements and pre-conditions for the success of the new talks. I discount much of these. But I do attach importance to convincing the Soviet leadership that we in the West are indeed serious in our aim of maintaining strategic stability at significantly lower levels of nuclear weapons. We do not want to give them the impression that we have something else in mind. We are serious about arms control. And we must be seen and heard to be so.

Finally, as members of the Atlantic Alliance, we must consider the potential consequences for this unique relationship. We must be sure that the US nuclear guarantee to Europe would indeed be enhanced as a result of defensive deployments. Not only enhanced at the end of the process, but from its very inception.

Many years of deployments may be involved. Many years of insecurity and instability cannot be our objective. All the allies must continue at every stage to share the same sense that the security of NATO territory is indivisible. Otherwise the twin pillars of the alliance might begin to fall apart.

Other things being equal, we welcome any cost-effective enhancement of deterrence to meet palpable weaknesses on the Western side. But we also have to consider what might be the offsetting developments on the Soviet side, if unconstrained competition in ballistic missile defences beyond the ABM Treaty limits were to be provoked. In terms of NATO's policy of forward defence and flexible response, would we lose on the swings whatever might be gained on the roundabouts?

I have posed a lengthy list of questions, to which the answers cannot be simple. Some do not admit of answers now. But that does not acquit us of the duty to pose them. They are questions so vital to our future that we cannot afford to shrug them off. It is right to ponder and debate them as research continues. In this way we stand the best chance of reaching the right policies. The attractions of moving towards a more defensive strategy for the prevention of war are as apparent as are the risks. It would be wrong to rule out the possibility on the grounds that the questions it raises are too difficult.

But the fact that there are no easy answers, that the risks may outweigh the benefits, that science may not be able to provide a safer solution to the nuclear dilemma of the past forty years than we have found already— all these points underline the importance of proceeding with the utmost deliberation. . . .

Deterrence has worked. And it will continue to work. It may be enhanced by active defences. Or their development may set us on a road that diminishes security. We do not know the answer to that question. Meanwhile, four clear points emerge.

First, as the Prime Minister reminded the United States Congress last month, in the words of Sir Winston Churchill: "Be careful above all things not to let go of the atomic weapon until you are sure, and more than sure, that other means of preserving peace are in your hands."

Secondly, impressions can be created by words as well as deeds. Policies, aims, visions—all these can and must be clearly stated. Without the approval of an informed public, the governments of the West are wasting their breath. But we must be especially on our guard against raising hopes that it may be impossible to fulfil. We would all like to think of nuclear deterrence as a distasteful but temporary expedient. Unfortunately we have to face the harsh realities of a world in which nuclear weapons exist and cannot be disinvented. Words and dreams cannot by themselves justify what the Prime Minister described to the United Nations as the "Perilous Pretence" that a better system than nuclear deterrence is within reach at the present time.

Thirdly, any deployments of space-based or other defences must be a matter for negotiation. The Prime Minister agreed about this with President Reagan at Camp David, and they reaffirmed it in Washington. In the words of the White House statement of 3 January, "Deployments of defensive systems would most usefully be done in the context of a cooperative, equitable and verifiable arms control environment. A unilateral Soviet deployment of such defences . . . would destroy the foundation on which deterrence has rested for twenty years." . . .

There is a fourth factor: the linkage between offensive and defensive systems. The White House statement of 3 January recognised the merit in controlling both the offensive and defensive developments and deployments on both sides. If defensive systems are to be deployed, they will be directed against the then levels of offensive forces. If the latter can be lowered dramatically, then the case for active defences may be correspondingly strengthened. Conversely, radical cuts in offensive missiles might make the need for active defences superfluous. Equally, the effectiveness of defences will be directly governed by the numbers of missiles and warheads which they are intended to destroy. If the levels rise dramatically, then the effectiveness of defences may not be adequate.

It is therefore clear that there is and will continue to be an integral relationship between measures to control offensive forces and any decisions to move to the development of active defences. The US administration have always recognised such a linkage. Belatedly, the Russians now seem to have reached the same conclusion. . . . A key question for all our futures will be the extent to which reductions in offensive forces prove possible and the impact this will have upon the incentive to develop defences. . . .

CHAPTER 19

Statement
to the Bundestag

Helmut Kohl

. . . Anyone who seriously desires a comprehensive reduction of nuclear weapons in the world and who harbors reservations against the strategy of nuclear deterrence should most carefully consider preventing war. Every option for getting away from using the menace of a nuclear holocaust as the final means to prevent war deserves conscientious examination.

Even today, no one can judge with certainty whether the U.S. President's SDI will prove to be the way to drastically reduce and ultimately ban nuclear weapons. However, ladies and gentlemen, if this course proves to be practicable, then historical merit will have to be accorded to Ronald Reagan.

Despite all debates on daily politics and the understandable differences of opinion that characterize democracy, all of us should seriously and farsightedly consider political visions if these visions can possibly bring us closer to the vital objectives of our policy.

. . . It is also not surprising to me or the Federal Government and the alliance that from the outset the Soviet Union has attacked and characterized as diabolical the U.S. defense initiative. The utter lack of truth and moral justification of these Soviet attacks is illustrated by the fact that for more than a decade now, the Soviet Union has itself been conducting, at considerable expense, comparable research on a widespread antimissile system. This is demonstrated by the fact that it is the only one of the two superpowers that has installed and continuously modernizes an operational antimissile system around its capital of Moscow.

In addition, the Soviet Union is the only country in the world that has operational antisatellite weapons . . . and by building a larger radar facility near Krasnoyarsk, it proves its determination—possibly in violation of the ABM treaty—to hold open for itself the option of a strategic defense. . . .

The U.S. SDI is a long-term research program that will extend far into the nineties. . . . Research on space systems is compatible with the ABM

Excerpted from the text of a statement to the Bundestag on the U.S. SDI, April 18, 1985.

treaty. There will not and cannot be automatic transition from research to development and deployment in connection with strategic defense systems. All decisions that go beyond the research program will be made only on the basis of proven research results. . . .

. . . The U.S. research program is from our point of view justified, politically necessary, and serving the security interests of the West as a whole. Consequently, the Federal Government supports the principle of the U.S. SDI program.

On 9 February 1985, at the Munich military science meeting, I outlined for the first time the significant elements of our position toward the U.S. project. I made it perfectly clear at that time that the decisive criterion of our assessment of the U.S. defense initiative is the question of whether this initiative can make peace in freedom more secure for us. . . .

. . . Our aim to create peace with increasingly fewer weapons and to develop more stability in East-West relations is naturally valid and unchanged. This is also the guideline for our policy toward the U.S. SDI project.

The interests of the FRG and of the West European allies are involved in the U.S. SDI project in many complex ways. We will be most deeply involved in possible political-strategic effects. These will have direct consequences for our most vital political interest, namely our external security. From the very beginning we must make a number of strategic demands, based not least of all on our geostrategic position.

In my speech in Munich, I pointed out very clearly that Europe's security must not be detached from that of the United States. There must be no zones of differing security levels within NATO. NATO's strategy of flexible response must continue to be valid in an unchanged way as long as no alternative is found that would promise to prevent war. We must avoid instability during any transitional phase from a strategy of pure deterrence to a new form of strategic stability based more firmly on defensive systems. Disparities must be removed and the development of new areas of threats below the nuclear level must be avoided.

. . . The connection between the political-strategic and arms control points of view is of special significance for us in assessing SDI. From a short- and medium-range point of view, adherence to the ABM treaty must have priority. In the Federal Government's view, it is imperative that, prior to decisions going beyond research, cooperative solutions must be sought that will guarantee that strategic stability will be preserved and, if possible, improved, that nuclear offensive weapons will be drastically reduced and that the ratio between offensive and defensive systems will be defined in a way that will guarantee as much stability as possible with as small a number of weapons as possible.

Together with its closest European allies, the Federal Government will energetically undertake efforts to develop a common stance on the U.S. SDI project. . . .

. . . In this connection, the Federal Government welcomes the French proposal conveyed by Foreign Minister Dumas early this week to Minister

Genscher that closer European cooperation in the field of future technologies be immediately initiated. I share the French Government's assessment that Europe's reply to the U.S. SDI program cannot consist of a policy of surrender or uncoordinated rejection.

I am happy that in our basic assessment of the U.S. SDI we are in agreement with Italian Prime Minister Craxi, British Prime Minister Thatcher, and other European partners.

We are open to the U.S. proposal to jointly study possibilities for participation in the research project. Participation of the European countries would be a historic opportunity for Europe to bring its political, strategic, and technological interests to bear as a community.

. . . Ladies and gentlemen, in this manner the U.S. SDI program could provide a real opportunity for the NATO alliance and for Europe, and could essentially contribute to strengthening the integration of the two. In view of the magnitude of funding—about DM80 billion—with which the U.S. Government plans to support its research program, it is quite evident to everyone even now that important and far-reaching results will be achieved—results whose significance, including the economic importance, will go far beyond the sphere of strategic defense. In this connection, the remark about the promotion of technological innovation on a broad basis is definitely no exaggeration.

Ladies and gentlemen, we will and must also be interested in utilizing research results in our industry that will have revolutionary civilian applications. Let me add, however, that it is not this economic-technological interest alone that will determine our decision on participating in the research program, but we must ensure that the FRG and West Europe are not outdistanced technologically and thus become second rate. As expressed in the alliance commitments, shared security between the United States and Europe also requires a comparable level of economic and technological developments in the United States and Europe.

Technological cooperation in the U.S. research project would make it easier for the FRG and our European allies to retain, and even increase, our influence on and importance in the major questions concerning the further development of alliance strategy. In the foreseeable future, the Federal Government will have to make a decision on participation in the research project. In making this decision, it will not tolerate being put under time pressure by anyone and will gather all the necessary information to make its decision.

To this end, essentially three measures have been envisaged: the Federal Government will discuss with the German economic sector its interest in and possibilities for participation in research, and, in so doing, also examine beginnings of cooperation among European companies. It will enter into consultations with interested European allies—particularly France, Great Britain, and Italy, but also with the other interested European partners— on a common definition of a stance and, if the occasion arises, on participation. The Federal Government will send a group of experts to the United States to ascertain the conditions and areas for participation in research. . . .

Ladies and gentlemen, let me sum up. The U.S. research program triggered by SDI is justified and is in the interests of the West as a whole. The U.S. SDI program constitutes an opportunity to further develop on a long-term basis the currently absolutely necessary deterrence with the threat of mutual annihilation through a strategy that rests more strongly on defensive elements and that would allow a comprehensive reduction of nuclear weapons. Nobody knows at this time whether this hope can come true, yet a no to this project at this time—and I am addressing this remark not least of all to you, ladies and gentlemen of the SPD—would not be in keeping with the responsibility that we also bear for our country's future.

The strategic stability between East and West and the unity of the alliance in the political and strategic respect must be guaranteed. The NATO strategy of flexible response remains valid and unchanged as long as there is no alternative that would better serve the objective of preventing war. The arms control function of SDI is of central importance to us. We will persistently advocate this approach to our U.S. allies. A drastic reduction of the nuclear offensive systems on both sides remains our prime objective.

The assessment of the U.S. initiative from the viewpoint of alliance policy makes evident the task of averting risks and purposefully utilizing existing opportunities through the cohesion of the alliance and through intensified exertion of influence by the European allies. Ladies and gentlemen, whoever says no today will not remove the risk for the alliance and will be unable to take advantage of existing opportunities. . . .

CHAPTER 20

Press Conference

Margaret Thatcher

Prime Minister: . . . President Reagan and I have had a very thorough and extensive discussion of the prospects for arms control negotiations. In the course of which we also naturally touched on the Strategic Defence Initiative. I was not surprised to discover that we see matters in very much the same light. I told the President that I have made it absolutely clear to Mr. Gorbachev that there was no question of the Soviet Union being able to divide the United Kingdom from the United States on these matters. Wedge-driving is just not on (exclamation mark)

I told the President of my firm conviction that the SDI research programme should go ahead. Research is, of course, permitted under existing United States/Soviet treaties, and we, of course, know that the Russians have already their research programme and that in the United States' view that programme has in some respects already gone beyond research.

We agreed on four specific points:

First, the United States and Western aim was not to achieve superiority, but to maintain balance, taking account of Soviet developments.

Second, that SDI-related deployment would, in view of treaty obligations, have to be a matter for negotiations.

Third, the overall aim is to enhance, and not to undermine, deterrence, and

Fourth, East-West negotiation should aim to achieve security with reduced levels of offensive systems on both sides.

This will be the purpose of the resumed United States/Soviet negotiations on arms control, which I warmly welcome.

Ladies and gentlemen, your questions. . . .

Question: Prime Minister, there seems to have been a distinction drawn by your government between support for research of space defence systems and support for testing or eventual deployment of such systems. The administration, through its spokes-people has made it clear, and through the Secretary of Defence, that it supports both those concepts, eventual

---

Excerpted from the text of a press conference at Andrews Air Force Base, December 22, 1984.

deployment and support for testing as well as research. Do you support both, or just research?

Prime Minister: I think you will find that question is dealt with in the four points which I gave you.

First, you have to do the research as a matter of balance. I indicated that the Soviet Union has already done some research and, indeed, she has already got an anti-satellite satellite capability. And, as you know, she has done a great deal of research on lasers and electronic pulse beams, and also, as you know, she appears to have some very special radars and has not, in fact, let us have the results of some of her nuclear testing, in accordance with agreement. So she has gone ahead on some of these matters and the United States has to do research as a matter of balance. Otherwise the Soviet Union would get ahead.

Now, research is within existing agreements. If the result of research is such that it is decided to go ahead with production and deployment, that has to be a matter for negotiation before those deployments could take place, because the deployments would be covered by treaty obligations.

So, first the research, which can be done without infringing the treaties, and I think it best to wait for the results of that research before being able to go any further or to conjecture about what would happen then. We know that we would have to go to negotiations then. . . .

Question: Prime Minister, are you concerned that a spirited U.S. research programme might fuel a process of competition that would lead to the militarization of space, which you have said you are concerned about? Is there such a thing as pure research?

Prime Minister: I have already indicated that the Soviet Union was ahead on anti-satellite satellites and we believe is very advanced on lasers and electronic pulse beams, and as you know, has these very very big radars and as you know, has more experience of anti-ballistic missile systems, because she deployed one in Moscow, than we have.

It is necessary, therefore, to embark upon a process of research on these matters really in order for the United States to keep balance and not to let the Soviet Union get ahead, so if your question is do you think that is going to fuel problems, then my answer is: already there must be problems because of the way in which the Soviet Union has an anti-satellite capability greater than we have. . . .

Question: Prime Minister, are you saying that as a result of today's talks there is no disagreement whatever with the administration on the issue of SDI and Star Wars weapons?

Prime Minister: I have indicated in great detail that I fully approve— and have long before I came here—and have said so long before I came here—that I think it right to go ahead on the research programme. There were, in fact, no differences and why I have made it abundantly clear today is that I have been concerned about reports to the effect that there were. Those reports were not correct. . . .

Question: Did you get the impression that Gorbachev was willing to walk out of the talks or would not even begin to talk if he felt the United States would not give on testing?

Prime Minister: No, we were not in that amount of detail. But I think it is absurd—if I might respectfully say so—to talk of walking out before the talks have even started and if I might turn one of the questions on you: do you not think that such a comment might fuel trouble? . . .

Look. The fact is that we have had peace in Europe for, next year, 40 years. That is a very long period of peace compared with previous periods. Historically, I believe that the deterrence of nuclear weapons and the fact that their use would be so horrific has, in fact, helped to keep that peace. That kind of deterrence is the policy that we are going to have to live with for some time, because the research will take some time to complete and I think you are probably referring to Secretary Weinberger's speech. I think, if you look, you will find three occasions in that speech when he pointed out that this was a feasibility study and it would take a long time before we could get all of the options worked out. So we are going to have to live with that same doctrine for a considerable time.

Question: What issues would need to be negotiated before any further SDI hardware would be deployed?

Prime Minister: Well, once you come into making the requisite weapons, then you are bound by the Anti-Ballistic Missile Treaty of 1972—I think the ABM Treaty is not limited by time—and you are also bound by I think it is the 1967 Treaty on Outer Space, and therefore you have, if there is any question of deployment, if the research indicated that deployment should go ahead, you then have to start to negotiate with the Soviet Union on that deployment. Otherwise, you would be in breach of treaty obligations and I do not believe that it is the intention to be in breach of treaty obligations on the part of the United States in any way.

Bibliography: Part Five

Boutwell, Jeffrey, and F. A. Long. "The SDI and U.S. Security." In Franklin A. Long, Donald Hafner, and Jeffrey Boutwell, eds., *Weapons in Space*. New York: Norton, 1986.

Freedman, Lawrence. "The 'Star Wars' Debate: The Western Alliance and Strategic Defence: Part II." *Adelphi Paper*, No. 199. London: International Institute for Strategic Studies, 1985, pp. 34–50.

Heseltine, Michael. "Strategic Defence Initiative," statement in the House of Commons, December 10, 1985.

Hoffman, Fred S. "The 'Star Wars' Debate: The Western Alliance and Strategic Defence: Part I." *Adelphi Paper*, No. 199. London: International Institute for Strategic Studies, 1985, pp. 25–33.

Lellouche, Pierre. "SDI and the Atlantic Alliance." *SAIS Review* (summer-fall 1985):67–80.

Wörner, Manfred. "A Missile Defense for NATO Europe." *Strategic Review* (winter 1986):13ff.

Glossary

Boost phase. The portion of a missile flight during which the payload is accelerated by the large rocket motors. For a multiple-stage rocket, boost phase involves the first two stages.

Chemical laser. A laser in which chemical action is used to produce the pulses of coherent light.

Coherent light. Light in which the effects of each photon build on top of others. A laser produces coherent light and therefore can concentrate energy.

Decoy. A device constructed to look and behave like a nuclear-weapon-carrying warhead but is far less costly and much less massive and can be deployed in large numbers to complicate defenses.

Directed energy. Energy in the form of particle or laser beams that can be sent long distances at nearly the speed of light.

Discriminate. The process of observing a set of attacking objects and determining which are the real warheads and which are decoys and other nonthreatening objects.

Electromagnetic gun. A gun based on the idea of an open solenoid. The projectile is accelerated by electromagnetic forces rather than by an explosion, as in a conventional gun.

Excimer laser. A chemical laser that uses noble gases, for example, helium, argon.

Intercept. The act of destroying a target.

Laser. A device for generating coherent visible or infrared light.

Leakage. The percentage of warheads that get through a defensive system intact and operational.

Neutral-particle beam. An energetic beam of neutral atoms (no net electric charge). A particle accelerator moves the particle to nearly the speed of light.

Particle beam. A stream of atoms or subatomic particles (electrons, protons, or neutrons) accelerated to nearly the speed of light.

Terminal phase. The final phase of a ballistic missile trajectory, during which warheads and penetration aids reenter the atmosphere.

About the Contributors

Lt. General James A. Abrahamson is director of the Strategic Defense Initiative Organization. He was associate administrator for the space transportation system, headquarters, NASA, prior to assuming his current position.

Christoph Bertram is foreign and political editor for *Die Zeit*. He was director of the International Institute for Strategic Studies in London from 1974 to 1982.

Harold Brown is chairman of the Foreign Policy Institute, School of Advanced International Studies of The Johns Hopkins University. He was president of the California Institute of Technology from 1969 to 1977, and secretary of defense from 1977 to 1981.

McGeorge Bundy was special assistant to the president for National Security Affairs from 1961 to 1966 and president of the Ford Foundation from 1966 to 1979. He is now professor of history at New York University.

Sidney D. Drell is professor and deputy director, Stanford Linear Accelerator Center, and co-director, Center for International Security and Arms Control, Stanford University.

Philip J. Farley is senior research associate at the Center for International Security and Arms Control at Stanford University.

James C. Fletcher is administrator of the National Aeronautics and Space Administration.

Mikhail S. Gorbachev is general secretary of the Communist party of the Soviet Union.

Colin S. Gray is president of the National Institute for Public Policy in Fairfax, Virginia.

Fred S. Hoffman is the director of Pan Heuristics in Marina del Rey, California.

David Holloway is senior research associate at the Center for International Security and Arms Control at Stanford University.

Sir Geoffrey Howe is the secretary of state for foreign and commonwealth affairs of the United Kingdom.

George F. Kennan is professor emeritus at the Institute for Advanced Study, Princeton University. He was director of the State Department Policy Planning Staff from 1947 to 1950. Other foreign service assignments included minister-counselor in Moscow in 1944, ambassador to the Soviet Union in 1952, and ambassador to Yugoslavia from 1961 to 1963.

George A. Keyworth II was science adviser to the president and director of the Office of Science and Technology Policy from 1981 to 1985. He is currently chairman of The Keyworth Company in Washington, D.C.

Helmut Kohl is chancellor of the Federal Republic of Germany.

Robert S. McNamara was secretary of defense from 1961 to 1968 and president of the World Bank from 1968 to 1981.

Paul H. Nitze is special adviser to the president and secretary for Arms Reduction Negotiations. He was a member of the U.S. SALT delegation from 1969 to 1974; assistant secretary of defense from 1967 to 1969; secretary of the Navy from 1963 to 1967; and director of the State Department Policy Planning Staff, 1950 to 1953.

George Rathjens is professor of political science at Massachusetts Institute of Technology. He has served as chief scientist and deputy director of the Defense Department's Advanced Research Projects Agency, special assistant to the director of the U.S. Arms Control and Disarmament Agency, and director of the Institute for Defense Analyses' Systems Evaluation Division.

Ronald Reagan was elected to his second term as president of the United States in 1984.

Jack Ruina is professor of electronic engineering at Massachusetts Institute of Technology. He has served as director of the Defense Department's Advanced Research Projects Agency.

Gerard Smith was chief of the U.S. delegation to the Strategic Arms Limitation Talks from 1969 to 1972. He served as special assistant to the secretary of state for atomic energy affairs, director of the State Department

Policy Planning Staff, ambassador at large, and special presidential representative.

Edward Teller is a senior research fellow at the Hoover Institution and associate director emeritus of the Lawrence Livermore National Laboratory. A recipient of the National Medal of Science, he serves on the White House Science Council.

Margaret Thatcher is prime minister of the United Kingdom.